TANGLED UP
IN WHITE

TANGLED UP IN WHITE

PETER ROEBUCK
ON CRICKET

Hodder & Stoughton
LONDON SYDNEY AUCKLAND

British Library Cataloguing in Publication Data

Roebuck, Peter
  Tangled up in white.
  I. Title
  796.358

  ISBN 0-340-56618-3

First published in Great Britain 1992

Reproduced by arrangement with William Heinemann Australia

Published by Hodder and Stoughton,
a division of Hodder and Stoughton Ltd,
Mill Road, Dunton Green, Sevenoaks, Kent TN13 2YA.
Editorial Office: 47 Bedford Square, London WC1B 3DP.

Photoset by Rowland Phototypesetting Ltd,
Bury St Edmunds, Suffolk.

Printed in Great Britain by
St Edmundsbury Press Ltd, Bury St Edmunds, Suffolk.

CONTENTS

Contents

Two Originals

SOMETHING FELL FROM HEAVEN

GRADUALLY the ball descended, obeying Newton's law. No snow on it, for the day was warm. The batsman waited and watched. Eventually he smote at it vigorously, with all the might he could muster. But he was deceived; the ball had not yet arrived. As he completed his lusty swing, the ball bounced and trickled towards the stumps. A bail was dislodged before the agonised batsman could retrieve his dignity. Another victim for Teer, another fool rushing in. As the disconsolate batsman trudged to the pavilion he muttered under his breath (as Agatha Christie victims mutter mysterious dying words), 'Something fell from heaven.'

Norman Teer bowls donkey-drops. He's been at it a long time, and with considerable success. He launches the ball far into the skies and then relaxes, awaiting the outcome. Something usually happens. His proud boast is to be 'the highest bowler in Somerset', though he concedes that Joel Garner is the tallest. His deliveries, sent into orbit from 24 yards, after a brief skip or two, soar at least 15 feet into the air. Once in a while he slips in a quicker ball which rises to only twice the height of man. In Gambia his deliveries often bounced over the batsman's head. Horrified Gambians were dumbfounded by this yo-yo style of bowling, and fell in droves. When it bounces, if it bounces, his donkey-drop will spin a little. That's an unnecessary touch. Probably Nureyev could sing, too, but who needs it?

From this you may gather that Norman Teer is an original, a remnant of more generous cricketing days. Every ball is a challenge, miserly efforts at run-saving are ignored. It's wickets that matter. Once in a while, say in a 30-over game, Norman's figures of five overs, three for 53, appear a bit of a luxury. But then, like most bowlers of his kind, Norman is captain, selector and organiser of his club, the Mendip Acorns. In these roles he usually manages to conclude that he should bowl, if not all the time, at least a good deal of it. He took well over 100 wickets in

1980, including several bags of '7 for' and '6 for'. One does not ask '7 for what?' or '6 for what?'

With these numerous wickets, a northern dialect, a balding patch and an air of immensely serious intent, one might imagine that Norman's deliveries contain a measure of guile, a touch or two of the wisdom gathered over the years by this sprightly 65-year-old. Not so. Norman is beyond wisdom. His philosophy is simple. 'They can't resist 'em, y'know,' he confides to uninitiated team-mates. And they can't. Norman arrives at the crease, orders his troops to disappear in various directions (mostly leading to the leg-side boundary) and measures his skip. Up floats the ball. Each delivery is a potential incident. A six, a four, a brilliant stop or a wicket. 'Dots' are few and far between. Maidens come about once a year (I'm told the position is similar in Cardiff).

At Paulton, in a match reduced to 12 overs, things were going badly. The ball was wet and no-one could grip it. Zaheer was playing for the Acorns. He had a bowl but his over cost him 12 runs. So Norman came on into the wind. Norman hates bowling into the face of even a gentle breeze. His first ball climbed as high as usual. The batsman advanced to dispatch it. He swung the bat but missed the ball. It rolled slowly towards the stumps. Recovering his wits, the batsman rushed back to his crease and put his foot behind the barely moving ball. Norman, ever keen for wickets, appealed for lbw. The umpire ruled in his favour. The batsman was stunned, shouting down the pitch, 'The ruddy ball wouldn't even have reached the ruddy wicket!' But he went his weary way in the end.

Things do happen when Norman is bowling. On another famous occasion, this time in Tavistock, Norman was being hit to the leg-side boundary rather frequently by an aggressive left-hander. Norman thereupon sent all his fieldsmen to the affected area (as sandbags are sent to help stem floods). The left-hander, espying the field, shrewdly decided to drive the ball to the cover boundary. He succeeded only in destroying his stumps, sending pieces of wood flying in all directions. Once again fielders fell about in helpless mirth as a furious batsman retraced his steps, trying to think of a convincing story to tell his captain.

If these incidents suggest that Norman Teer plays in a low standard of cricket, they are misleading: the Mendip Acorns have included Zaheer, Underwood, Vivian Richards and Don

Shepherd amongst their numbers. But to resist Norman's bait is not merely a matter of ability; it requires humility. It is the devil tempting Jesus on the hill. Pride demands that he must be hit for six, for how can one be a man and yet collect gentle singles off these skyscrapers? No, no red-blooded man could resist the challenge. Let the voice of caution be still awhile, let the boundary fielders be alert. Alas, the boundary is well staffed, and it is not so easy to hit such slow balls for six. And so numerous self-respecting batsmen succumb, falling into the trap as knowingly as lemmings fall into the sea.

Norman derives enormous pleasure from watching opponents fall prey to his wiles. He loves his cricket in all its variations; the more improbable the venue, the more outlandish the game, the better. He has organised many overseas tours for his club, 25 in the past 12 years. Sierra Leone, the West Indies, Malta and the Far East have all been visited – not bad for an apparently innocuous tyre salesman.

That frail, *Diary of a Nobody* appearance is deceptive. Norman is a talented organiser. His tourists have included opera singers, academics, bookmakers and mechanics. The tyre business is a side-show, an excuse to spend a day by the phone arranging another tour. His only concession to the exigencies of business is to encourage Acorns to buy Teer's tyres (Teer's tyre pressure, it is called), just as Al Capone encouraged clients to buy his liquor. Nor is Norman as shy as he looks. Startled Acorns often emerge from a plane to be greeted by dignitaries, steel bands and dancing girls. In Barbados, Dr Eric Glair, by all accounts a formidable man, met the Acorns. ''Morning, Eric,' ventured our intrepid leader. Mr Teer has the hide of a hippo and the nerve of an unhelmeted batsman. He needs it, to bowl like that.

Acorns' cricket is deadly serious, particularly on tour. Humour arises from a haphazard series of events, from an improbable combination of individuals (for Acorns' teams include examples of all shapes, hues, ages and abilities). It is not forced, the cricket is not for fun. Often the humour is unconscious. There is nothing necessarily funny about Norman Teer and Derek Underwood bowling in harness. Yet in the West Indies in 1971 they were a hugely popular pairing. Quite what Deadly Derek made of it all one can only speculate. It was not long before local radio stations were providing running descriptions of the game, with commentators in danger of falling from their lofty perches as hilarity increased. By the end of the tour people were coming from miles around to study this extraordinary bowler. Norman was a hero. Not that he was impressed in the slightest by all this fuss. He wheeled away with a lot of flight and a bit of guile, watching with a perplexed air as the ball soared over the boundary, or explaining the subtleties of each wicket with the aplomb of Trueman in his prime.

For all the cheerful optimism of his bowling, Norman is immensely competitive. Woe betide any fielder who misses a chance off his bowling. Any ball hit in the air brings forth the view that the nearest beggar should have caught it. Possibly Norman does not select enough beggars. Once, amidst the usual tirade of hooks, cuts, drives and sweeps, a batsman popped up a ball into the vacant short-leg position. Captain Teer sidled up to me at the completion of the over and said, 'I knew I should have put someone there.' Volunteers for the forward short-leg position to Norman Teer might have been few and far between in a team of VCs, I suspect.

As a cricketer Norman is, you may agree, colourful and imaginative. He is also not beyond a little deviousness. It is darkly whispered that Acorns teams are chosen so as to include plenty of batting and a scarcity of bowling. As the team gathers, Norman (the man who selected the team) sometimes peers around his players and discovers, to his apparent dismay, that he has no opening bowlers. 'Better open up myself,' he concludes. Once this ploy worked well. Bowling the first over to a proficient batsman, Norman sent all his fielders to the boundary and served up a juicy slow long hop. The opener duly smote it fiercely back to the bowler. It landed in our hero's stomach, knocking him to the ground. He clung to the ball, rising in triumph as he dusted himself, to explain, 'I knew he'd do that.'

Despite all the batsmen in his team, Norman often discovers, to his evident astonishment, that 'though our batting is strong, we don't appear to have a second opener'. Whereupon he straps on his pads and cuts and carves successfully until Cyril or Archie, well used to Teer's way, judge their President to be lbw.

Despite advancing years, I expect Norman will continue for a long while. 'Just one more tour,' he repeats from time to time, much as Frank Sinatra would say, 'Just one more concert.' Anyhow, he still has one ambition left: to travel to a game on a camel. The Acorns are presently planning a tour to Bahrain.

BRIAN CLOSE

Many colourful characters have adorned Somerset cricket. From Sammy Woods and Jack White to Bill Andrews and Arthur Wellard, from Bill Alley and Colin McCool to Close and Botham, Somerset has been enriched by provocative, unpredictable men. Brian Close, the 'bald old blighter' as Alan Gibson dubbed him, or 'The Godfather' as we called him, brought to Taunton a fierce individualism and an uncompromising will to win.

He came when his best cricketing days were behind him, when a topsy-turvy career was gradually coming to its end. Those last few seasons were as explosive, as turbulent as most of the others. Brian Close left cricket not with a whimper, but with a bang. He retired in 1977 still cursing, still gritting his teeth, still trying to belt balls over deep mid-wicket, still standing at short leg giggling and glaring. We missed him when he left and realised how much we had enjoyed his personality, for all its impulsiveness.

Brian Close left a fund of anecdotes in his wake. His total commitment and his originality ensured that life was never dull under his leadership. Close took chances as a captain and as a man. He did not put long leg at long leg, he moved him 17 feet in and a little wider than usual. You see, he'd had this vision of what was going to happen and he arranged his field accordingly. You'd find yourself fielding in no-man's-land, wondering whether you ought to be a bit closer or just a touch deeper, feeling uneasy. But you'd stay put, just in case the Old Blighter was right. And you'd stay in exactly the correct place, having scraped a large mark in the ground to define your position. Then if there was a disaster, at least you could point feebly to your scrape. Alas, Close could move you around a touch here, a hint there, so you ended up with a series of crosses resembling a pools coupon.

But woe betide you if you strayed from your position, especially if truth enacted the vision. After an unusually ungenerous declaration, Close's victory drive was being easily thwarted by the Essex batsmen. Nevertheless he deployed his troops with minute attention to detail, fiercely clapping his hands at short leg at the merest hint of relaxation. As the players went through the final rites of a stalemated game, Hardie drove a skimming chance to Steve ('Aggro') Wilkinson at mid-on. Aggro had slipped a yard or two too deep, moved too late and muffled the chance. It did not seem to matter, and stumps were drawn a few overs later. Everyone left the field content. Not Close: he stormed into the dressing room muttering, 'If = Aggro had caught that = catch we'd have beaten the =s.'

It was not in Close's nature to concede error easily. His best-laid plans were always being frustrated by someone's incompetence. His strength lay in the force of his convictions, the strength of his personality, nor in his ability to doubt his own judgement. He led by drive and inspiration. Sometimes these inspirations succeeded, other times they fell in ruins. Against Gloucestershire in a Benson and Hedges game Close introduced Mervyn Kitchen and Richard Cooper into the attack. No-one quite knew why. Neither of these rotund characters had bowled in public for several seasons. Kitchen trapped Ron Nicholls with a wide long hop. Nicholls was furious! Then Cooper, who contrived to bowl no-balls of a three-pace amble, persuaded Procter to sky a high full toss (Aussies call 'em head-hunters). Kitchen hovered under it awhile but sadly dropped the chance, amidst considerable swearing from short leg.

Richie Benaud, from the commentary box, hailed these manoeuvres as acts of genius. Nor did the drama end there. At lunch Close informed an already startled team that 'we're going to catch 'em unawares'. He proceeded to bowl out his best bowlers, leaving leg-spinners and medium-pacers to deliver the final 20 overs. Procter scored 150 and took 5 for 30, and Somerset lost by a mile. Yet how near success had been! Probably Brian Close's captaincy was more suited to the three-day game, which offers scope for flair and imagination, than to the essentially defensive limited-over matches in which gambles are usually luxuries.

Still, the Godfather was an extraordinary man, a mixture of King Lear storming in the wilderness and Churchill defying 'em on the beaches. An immensely strong man, too: as a youngster he used to sit in a sauna for half an hour (try it, at 100°), doing press-ups, burpees and the rest – now try that! He never doubted his own physical prowess. Watching an Ali v. Frazier fight, Close informed his colleagues that he could beat 'em both on the same night. And he was convinced, utterly convinced, that he could.

Not that Brian Close idly boasted of his abilities. His strength was tremendous, and it was more than matched by his courage. His leadership might have been erratic but it never lacked guts and drive. He might swear at his team, pursue some extraordinary tactic to its bitter end, yet he never lost his popularity as a man. You could tolerate a great deal from someone who fought so hard to win. His ordeal against Michael Holding at Old Trafford in 1976 demonstrated his resilience, his tenacious refusal at 45 years of age to back down one inch. It was as if his very manhood were being challenged. He allowed a succession of devastating deliveries to pound into his chest. He survived, bruised but not unbowed. I watched this terrifying episode of the BBC highlights that night. Graham Burgess and Mervyn Kitchen were in the hotel room, too. We were diving under the sheets as if it were a Hitchcock movie. And we were 100 miles away!

Less well-known is the postscript to the Old Trafford Test. Close played for Somerset in a Gillette Cup game next day. His chest was badly bruised. He was struck on it by Willis and buckled at the knees. Instantly he stood up again to continue his innings. It scarcely needs saying that he emerged as Somerset's top scorer that day.

But courage can be a dangerous friend. Close utterly refused to back down or to admit fault, whatever the weight of opinion might be. His attempts to sweep Benaud in 1961 were callously condemned by E. W. Swanton, yet regarded as worthwhile risks by Benaud. His loss of the England captaincy for his delaying tactics at Edgbaston followed his downright refusal to admit either that Yorkshire had prevaricated (to put it mildly!) or that prevarication was unfair. Ironically, and Brian Close's cricketing life was full of irony, Close had the previous winter suggested the implementation of a '20 overs in the final hour' rule. It was introduced one year too late to save his job. Somerset players will remember Close's lament, after rain had reduced Somerset's 1977 Gillette Cup semi-final against Middlesex to a 15-over farce and as he realised that his last chance of success had withered and died, that 'my life has been a series of cock-ups'.

Brian Close was not usually a self-analytical man. He did not grasp the humour of the things that happened to him. Stories about Close rely upon the image of the Old Blighter chewing gum, standing hands on knees at short leg, growling. His comment to Tom Cartwright, made as Gary Sobers walked out to bat, was not intrinsically hilarious. Yet everyone laughed uproariously at the time. Close strode knowingly to Cartwright, full of earthy wisdom and wily experience, and said as if it were a brilliant insight, 'Now, Tom, this lad's a left-hander!'

And at Torquay during a Sunday League game, Close informed his partner of his intention to swipe every ball bowled by Surrey's Michael Hooper to the invitingly short mid-wicket boundary. Two sixes were hit, so Hooper dropped one a shade shorter. Close swept massively, edging the ball into his mouth. Teeth and blood scattered everywhere. Close repaired to the dressing room, sipping whisky to dampen the pain. Next day he returned to Taunton to continue the Championship match. He sat miserably in his corner, grimacing with each shaft of pain, unable to eat or speak. Maurice Hill, who knew nothing of the injury, entered the room clutching his jaw and whispering 'Hellfire, I've got toothache this morning!' Bette Davis never matched Close's anguished glare at Hill.

A postscript to this story, too. Close scored a century that day.

These things happened to Brian Close. He had a reckless quality that attracted incident as the candle attracts the moth. Only Close could walk through a glass door (he did not notice it!) and escape unhurt as he did at Westcliff. Only Close could decide to keep wicket with bare hands in a vital Gillette Cup game (apparently the injured Jim Parks's gloves did not fit!).

Yet his 'damn the consequences' determination was not selfish. Close was not a mean-spirited man, he neither cheated nor passed harsh judgements. Well, not often at any rate. If an umpire handed down an unfavourable verdict a storm might follow. One umpire who did was described, a few minutes later, as 'a nice man, but he'll have to go, you know'. He's still with us!

It is said that Close only ever complained about pain once. In a hospital it was. He was having his shoulder put back in joint. He grumbled to the nurse that he was in agony, and the nurse rebuked him, saying, 'There's a mother upstairs having twins and she's not making a fuss.' To which Close retorted, 'Well, put them back in and see how she likes it!'

Despite these stories, Brian Close was not a figure of fun; far from it. He was not a humorous man in the least. He brought a hard core of competitive fight to Somerset. On the field he roared, cajoled, dived and jumped in his efforts to inspire victory. Yet off it, he was very much a loner. He stayed in a hotel room in Taunton, leaving his family in the North for the summer. He usually ate alone. Nor did he say much in the dressing room, living in a self-contained world of cricket and horses. Mostly he studied the *Sporting Life*, urging on various horses tipped by a mysterious figure known to us as 'Jackie Lad'. These animals invariably seemed to come second, often through incredible bad luck. As a result of this remoteness his team kept a respectful distance. Apart from the repeated request to 'fetch us a cup of tea, lad', Close remained not aloof, but a little removed. His stature, physical and mental, ensured that no liberties were taken.

Certainly you concentrated very, very hard if you were batting with him or fielding to his bowling. It was not wise to run him out. On his return to Yorkshire he received an emotional ovation from 10,000 admirers. It was somehow inevitable that he should soon be cursing and dusting off dirty whites, as he strode furiously back to the pavilion having been run out. And at Oxford poor Steve Wilkinson called, 'Yes, no, wait, sorry,' leaving Close sprawling on the turf having just scrambled to safety. He did not bother to rise; he turned a balding head and berated Aggro for a considerable time, a sight well worth seeing . . .

But, for all his foibles, a deep warmth for Close survives in cricket. He could not be matched for courage or inspiration. His unconscious humour and tough approach survives, too. In my first Championship game I scored 46. After my dismissal our chairman, Len Creed, approached Close and observed, 'Young Roebuck played well, didn't he, Brian?' To which our intrepid hero replied, 'Ah, Len lad, there you are. What have you got for the 3.30 at Plumpton?'

But he had been watching, you know. He told me, 'Well played, lad, but tha should have scored a century.'

CRICKET THE
WORLD OVER

MY ONLY CRICKET RIOT

Most cricketers have their riots in Karachi, Delhi or Jamaica. My riot took place in Corfu, just off the west coast of Greece.

I'd played cricket several times in Greece. I holiday there after every English cricket season and invariably end up playing somewhere for someone. In Athens we played on a dirt soccer pitch with a mat laid down in the middle of it. No effort was made to flatten the dirt; after all, the mat was flat! I was playing for a team raised by eccentric ex-Somerset captain R. J. O. Meyer. We were to play British Airways. Somerset bowler Colin Dredge was in our team (he was unimpressed by the Acropolis – 'Didn't think much of it. Couldn't live there, could you?') and bowled the first ball. It pitched on a good length, lifted and carried on lifting for some time as the slips and wicket-keeper watched it. It kept rising ever upward, eventually reaching the distant boundary second bounce. If that was his loosener . . . , we all thought. Colin was advised to bowl slow half-volleys. Needless to say, he was belted all around the ground.

Matting wickets can offer prodigious bounce. This prevents tall bowlers from hitting the stumps. Most Greek bowlers employ 'curly' actions, bowling from about shoulder height, threatening to clip the umpire's ear. They skim the ball down, hoping it will skid. This gives them the chance of clean bowling someone or appealing for lbw, and with Greek umpires it's not wise to be struck anywhere below the ribs!

Corfu is not quite as primitive as Athens. The square has a concrete strip in the middle, which ensures an even, bouncy wicket. The boundaries vary: on one side are the cafés and tavernas which attract the players and tourists with shade and Greek coffee. On the far side is a short grass boundary with a large car park behind it. The furthest edge of the car park is the boundary unless the ball hits a car or coach on its way, in which case four is signalled. Let me now introduce you to a favourite Corfiote tactic. When you bat there is not a car or coach to be seen and the boundaries are gigantic. During the interval (it couldn't be called Tea, for there is no tea, and 'Cappuccino' doesn't sound quite right), by mysterious magic the car park gradually fills until as you take the field it is full and the boundary 30 yards shorter! Incidentally this car park ploy works in reverse if the Corfiotes bat first. W. G. Grace would have been proud of it!

If the Corfiotes do field second, another tactic is available. No, not to ply the batsmen with ouzo or retsina – that's taken for granted – but slow over-rates. Night falls very quickly in those parts, so if you place the field with care and change it as often as possible, it can be dark just as the opposition are nearing your total.

They are not as naive as they pretend, these Corfiotes. After all, the Greeks produced Platonic philosophy, the Parthenon and Melbourne. Of course, all they really care about nowadays is politics and soccer. If an election is taking place in Athens, 600,000 people will meet in Sintagna Square on three successive nights for three different parties. And if they shout 'one' or 'two' it is not a call to run, it is delight at the fortunes of AEK, Olympiakos or Panathenaikos. By the way, the Greeks developed their language especially so as to confuse the English. 'OK' means 'no', 'nay' means 'yes'. We English tend to regard that sort of behaviour as Irish. Somerset players have been known to attempt similar things in benefit games, 'yes' meaning 'no', and 'no' 'yes'. The time to worry in that case is when your partner mutters 'slow down' as you pass!

Now, this riot. We were on our second trip to Corfu, having a terrific time. The previous year an individual named Pandreus had slaughtered our attack to score 126 in 20 overs, hitting some mighty blows over the hotels and tavernas. This time we were determined to beat Phaiax and Gymnasticos. Well, we beat Phaiax, notwithstanding cars, umpires, ouzo and donkeys wandering across the pitch with a perplexed air. For the Gymnasticos game we decided to infiltrate one of our own umpires, to even things up a bit.

They batted first, scoring 128 in 30 overs. Our openers, the usual sacrificial lambs, set about the chase. In the third over one of our men may (or may not) have tickled the ball to the 'keeper; 'just a faint one,' as the pros say. Now there is no rubbish about walking in Corfu: if they appeal you stand there looking indignant, rub your elbow and wave your arms about (not easy to do at the same time!). If this does not work, you mutter dark words and leave the field shaking your head.

Our man edged the ball, or missed it, and our hero in a white coat said 'not out', or 'OK out' as the Greeks put it. The bowler, a fierce Heathcliff type, grunted and bowled again. Our man swept him past square leg for four. That was a mistake, for the bowler went berserk. He grabbed a stump and chased our umpire around the field. This caused a certain amount of surprise. After a while the batsmen decided to help the umpire in distress. Thereupon the opposition, espying that the odds had now swung in favour of the visitors, joined in the mêlée. At about this time, those of us awaiting our turn at the crease rushed into the fray waving cricket bats, newspapers or Grecian urns.

The growing crowd enjoyed this spectacle enormously. 'Better than Spartacus,' someone exclaimed. Several American tourists thought it a substantial improvement on the cricket, though a couple of them assumed it was a natural part of the game. Maybe they'd seen Gaelic football in Dublin, which makes most riots look like peace marches. Of course the locals joined in; even Stan Bradley from Bolton joined in. (Stan was visiting Corfu trying to arrange a Brass Band Festival there. An optimist, Stan.) For a while it resembled a punch-up at the OK Corral, one of those where John Wayne is clobbering everyone before James Stewart stops the fight and puts everyone except John Wayne in jail.

I suppose it lasted in all about five minutes. For a while it was a bit tense, but a few ouzos restored international relations. Or perhaps it was Panathenaikos' victory which cheered everyone up. And I fancy the American tourists were right – the riot was much more fun than the cricket!

IN FIJI

THEY have some strange customs in Fiji, as I realised during my visit there. As usual I did not learn my lesson quite quickly enough to avoid trouble! After a day's cricket we repaired to a nearby tin shack, perched precariously on stilts, for a few drinks to whet our appetite for supper. A pig was smoking (not idly inhaling a Havana but roasting on a spit: I daresay the pig would have preferred the cigar). We sipped at our whisky with developing enthusiasm. To be honest, I mistrust the stuff; I've watched too many W. C. Fields films to feel at ease with it. Still, Fiji is a long way from home and they were downing scotches like Humphrey Bogart. These Fijians are men's men, built like Charles Bronson, moustache and all, and if they drink you must do so, too.

Although we had few words in common, conversation flourished as the scotch nagged away at empty stomachs, and with shrewd use of limbs, grunts and groans we were quickly deep in debate. It resembled one of those spaghetti westerns with Clint Eastwood and Lee Van Cleef in which growls, snarls and flickers express profound emotion. Eventually, I'm forced to concede, the pangs of hunger led me to deny my upbringing by asking whether the pig might not be well done by now. After all, we'd been sipping and chatting for hours, and I'd not eaten since that gigantic breakfast at half-noon (by this stage I was affecting a manner of expressing time reliant upon observation rather than Seiko, and drawn largely from Geronimo). And as we appeared to have two moons now, and as my stomach was rumbling, might we not bang the gong? Immediately they sprang to their feet. After a few wobbles they intimated that they'd been waiting for two hours for me to say I was hungry. Apparently in Fiji it is considered rude to dine until the guest gives the nod. With our different customs we could have been there all night.

My visit to Fiji was a trip into the unknown. I doubt if even Bing Crosby and Bob Hope ever went on the road there, from

an advanced material society to subsistence farming. Living in
tin shacks, without fridges or TV, was a way of life. Yet no-one
complained of hardship, all were well fed. No-one appeared to
be worried about anything although the Indian population, who
want things to run on time, looked wary. The Fijians can be
startlingly unreliable. If you arrange a match to begin at 2 pm
you might, with a little luck, find eight players by 3 pm. Everyone
will be immensely cheerful, sitting in the shade as the heat of
the day passes. As you fret, they smile. Maybe they had found
something better to do. Replacements are easy to find. Nip out
to the road, hail the first passing Pacific Islander (the Indians
take business more seriously) and enquire whether he fancies a
game of cricket? 'Sure,' he replies, delighted, and, after a pause,
'What's cricket?'

Usually these men, even the novices, contribute something to
the game. Superb athletes with massive shoulders, they all field
well and throw ferociously. It must be those strange root vegetables. At the wicket they will probably swipe a couple of mighty
blows before laughing uproariously as their stumps are spread-
eagled.

It's a pity, with this zest and delight, that cricket is dying in
Fiji. It has lost the enthusiasm and drive brought by the mission-
aries long ago. In older days Fiji could visit New Zealand, as
they did in 1948, and hold their own with provincial teams.
Even now the most senior cricketers bat with skill, evidently
well coached in the techniques of the science. Alas, most of the
youngsters are keen but undisciplined, in need of a stern ground-
ing in fundamentals. These youngsters might do well in familiar
conditions, but they struggle abroad. In the 1979 mini-World
Cup, Fiji brought a talented native team which fared very badly.
Of course the bitter, damp weather did not help. Nor did the
novelty of playing on grass and wearing cricket boots. Malo Bula,
a whimsical off-spinner, wore cricket whites for the first time in
Shrewsbury – previously he had preferred his native Sulu dress.
Not many Fijians wear Sulus, even though its thick cloth renders
pads virtually unnecessary. Most wear more orthodox attire, but
nevertheless first-class cricketers' eyebrows would bobble up and
down at the implements used in Fiji. Batsmen wear no helmet
or visor, chest protectors are not thought to be essential. Gloves
are too expensive and are scorned anyway. Several men, facing
bowlers of, say, Hendrick's pace, not only forswear helmets and

gloves but wear no shoes or socks either! A riveting sight.

Malo is quite a character, by the way, a cunning bowler who laughs and fools around too much to be a regular in his national side. A Fijian Ray East. To be too unreliable for Fiji! It's a bit like being rejected by Attila for being too ferocious.

Although cricket is battling to survive on the biggest islands of the Fiji group, it is thriving in one small and remote isle, Lakeba. Lakeba has a population of 2,500 comprising 32 different tribes. It is the home of Fiji's Prime Minister, Ratu Sir Kamisese Mara. Being a wise man, Sir Kamisese has forbidden the playing of rugby in Lakeba, since it caused far too many tribal injuries – a most judicious move, which the Welsh might bear in mind! Cricket, he felt, might result in less open warfare. So it was to Lakeba I flew, landing on a minute strip of sand, to see Fijian cricket at its best. Lakeba is a mixture of communal farming and mediaeval crafts. Each family has its role in the island's subsistence economy. One family organises everything, another traditionally runs the shop, another has always distributed the food, and everyone takes his turn working in the fields.

It is an unusual island, an improbable nest of cricket. The shy inhabitants stick together, reluctant to accompany outsiders in the Fiji team, proud of their heritage. Attitudes are similar to those found in Barbados, as the great traditions breed insularity. Mind you, Lakeba is not so very different from the rest of Fiji. It, too, runs, to a mysterious concept known as 'Fiji time'. This requires everyone to be at least two hours late. Every once in a while, though, and without any apparent signal, everyone must be half an hour early, just to show who is boss. It's a strange notion, inaccessible to guests, and you end up puzzled, shrugging your shoulders.

Matches in Lakeba are an event, the event to which every inhabitant looks forward. No need for ritual dances when you can appeal for lbw, no value in witch doctors when umpires and scorers are available. The whole island turns out for the games, played on Wednesdays (Sundays are reserved for less solemn religions). And, as one wide-eyed child put it, 'We all come, the blind, the crazy – even the teachers!' At first, dull-witted authorities in Suva decreed with dire threats that schools in Lakeba must stay open on Wednesdays. But no-one ever turned up, so, defeated, the Government withdrew gracefully.

The pitch is set, in village-green style, amongst the huts in which the locals live. Ratu Sir Kamisese Mara's house dominates one boundary and the sparkling Pacific laps into the palm trees on another. Lakebans sit under the palms skirting the ground, cheering, laughing, clapping. Heroes are not taken too seriously, not when you harvest alongside them in the fields. The pitch itself is made of concrete, covered by a thin green canvas. It is a reliable surface, encouraging batsmen to swing through the line. The ocean breeze assists swing-bowling. Nothing is done to aid spinners, for boundaries are short and canvas unreceptive. But then, visiting teams invariably rely on spin while Lakeba are stronger in pace and movement.

Incidentally, innocent visiting teams must be careful in these parts, must define the rules of the game with the utmost attention to detail. One team, *en route* to Lakeba, stopped on a nearby island for a quick game. Alas they did not realise that playing the island involved playing the *whole* island, men, women and children. People kept cheerfully strapping on pads and striding out to bat. No-one had the slightest idea how to swing a bat but every inhabitant wanted a go. It proved to be a long fielding session. You try to dismiss 170 men, women and children in an evening.

(Actually, novel views of cricket are not uniquely Fijian. Joe Hillaire, a colleague of mine at Cranbrook School, Sydney, believed that byes should not count since 'ze man did not hit ze ball'. Joe also kept score in a refreshingly different way. With Joe 3 for 48 meant you had dismissed three batsmen from 48 balls! George Gassman, our German teacher, on the other hand advised his lowly team to use the back of the bat so that the fielders would not know which way the ball was going! Meanwhile K. J. Lee, the resident Japanese, never could see quite why he needed to umpire from behind the stumps. Much more fun to stroll around the field, giving decisions from a variety of angles!)

Cricket is not nearly so distinctive in Lakeba. The proud Island team holds the national shield and most decidedly intends to keep it. The great hero, and a cricketer of explosive talent, is Peni Dakai. Peni resembles Andy Roberts, with his powerful shoulders and steely blue eyes. But though he does open the bowling with his swingers, his reputation rests on his batting, which can be as destructive as that of Roberts' Antiguan colleague, Vivian Richards. Peni hits the ball very, very hard. He lives at deep mid-wicket, which is appropriate enough, though he prefers to drive the ball over the trees into the ocean 100 yards away. His record in Lakeba includes several rapid centuries against reputable clubs. In England he was ever cold and depressed and gave only glimpses of his prowess. He survived only four balls against Bangladesh, but that was enough time for a 'sighter', a four and a skimming, straight six that almost broke the sight-screen. Peni is a hitter, not a slogger: like Richards, he uses a short back-lift and is a dangerous, powerful opponent. Had Dakai been born in a more mature cricketing country he might well have brightened our lives. How many other cricketers of genius are scattered around the world, unrecognised?

Despite the mysteries of Fiji time and mountainous English breakfasts, I survived my trip to Lakeba. I fear I resembled Sir Stafford Cripps in my coaching, though, as I tried to persuade these huge men to hit straight rather than to cow-shot corner (a phrase that took some explaining). At least I made no effort to restrict their natural joy in 'beating the ball'.

By the way, the smoked pig was delicious and the root vegetables restored my sorely tested strength. And I enjoyed the whisky, too!

ROEBUCK THE DEMON
BOWLER 1 (KOWLOON)

Wʜᴀᴛ a life! Well, I did have my day as a fast bowler. I still
have the press cuttings. The *Hong Kong Times*, carrying the story
just under the news of the Iraqi troops storming through Iran,
reported that 'Roebuck bowled fast and short, causing considerable discomfort.' Apparently my figures were 13–4–25–3. As
ever, dry statistics fail to reflect the colour of the day, as the
Times carried on, 'Two batsmen left the field with injuries after
being struck by rising deliveries from Roebuck.' Well, there you
are, see. Alas, a grave danger persists that this game might be
lost to posterity. And since you badger me for the details I must,
with due modesty and profound reluctance, bow to the overwhelming demand to describe the match.

You'll not be interested in our tepid innings. We, by the
way, were the Mendip Acorns on tour in Malaysia, Singapore
and Hong Kong. We were an improbable concoction of old,
young, able and golfer. We had already played Hong Kong
Cricket Club on its magnificent postage stamp ground in the
hills beyond the city. We had come second in that game. This
time we were facing Kowloon in the very heart of that crowded,
teeming city. We scored 150 or thereabouts. Nearby pools and
cocktails had proved much too attractive for long innings on
that scorching day. Young Dermot Reeve, Kowloon's fast
bowler, had flashed several bouncers past astonished nostrils.
Our attack, alas (and alack), consisted of Mervyn Kitchen
(a willing but ageing and rotund medium-pacer) and the
wicket-keeper. At slip it did seem that the world was a shabby,
unfair place in which to live. Where were our strapping quicks,
used to carrying sheep under each arm or, if not actually
eating coal, certainly cutting it, pick-axe in hand?

And then, as Jekyll turned into Hyde, so I became Fred Trueman, snorting and hissing. I growled to Kitchen (who was changing too, pink with sun, white with effort and wet with sweat) that
I wanted the ball. I marked my run. Eleven paces, enough for

Typhoon Tyson, enough for Holding on his short run. And quite enough for me after the previous night's activities. My first over was a range-finder, as Lieutenant Leslie Phillips's first navigational instruction in the *Navy Lark* (invariably a carefully weighed up 'left hand down a bit!') was an experiment not to be taken too literally. I was disconcerted to discover that the ball was swinging. I have enough trouble getting the ruddy thing straight as it is, without it veering off course when it is heading for the stumps. So this discovery, pleasing most bowlers, disturbed me.

As heat mounted, within and without, I strove for full pace. The broken down Ford Pop. purred as smoothly as a Renault. I let fly, hurling the ball down, flashing the ball past startled batsmen to our ageing reserve 'keeper, who hurled himself hither and thither like a jack-in-the-box.

Kowloon's batsmen were soon battered and bruised. I scarcely bowled a short ball (that's my story, and I'm sticking to it). They kept climbing steeply off a length, like Harrier jump-jets. I slipped one through an opener, to bring to the crease a not especially heroic Pakistani. He decided to swipe every half-volley, and to dive for cover every other ball. This caused a measure of merriment for a while, though no self-respecting hairy quick could tolerate this nonsense for long. So I lengthened my run, hurled down a ball with every ounce of strength I had, and Genghis Khan returned to the sanctuary of the pavilion. Another Pakistani entered the fray, a far most robust character. He defended sternly for a few overs before essaying an ambitious hook which landed on his stumps via his aggrieved chin. He smiled the smile of defeat, raised his cap and, with a 'good afternoon', left the field in regal dignity.

Next an Aussie strode to the crease, a tough little nugget well used to fiery games of cricket. He hooked his first ball for two, laughing scornfully as he passed me, as if to say, 'Is that as fast as you can bowl?' I felt insulted, like Wes Hall seeing Brian Close advance down the pitch, undaunted by fear. I'd nail the son of doubtful parentage. Alas, the Aussie fought hard and survived until tea, limbs and wickets intact. The energy-sapping heat had taken its toll. I climbed the stairs to tea wearily, braving the barrackers who disapproved of the tearaway blood-and-thunder fast bowler.

I tore off my damp shirt, revealing a Herculean chest, and

hung it (the shirt) over the railings to dry. I strolled imperiously to tea, aware of accusing stares. Hell, this is fun. No wonder Dennis Lillee doesn't retire.

CRICKET IN A COW PADDOCK

CRICKET is alive and well in Wanganui. This is only fairly good news for the Australian selectors, because as a place Wanganui would interest J. Edgar Hoover more than Messrs Sawle, Higgs and Benaud.

They had organised a game for Pioneer Day on Saturday and the *Herald* had decided to report the event. We found the place. Do not scoff at this. Last year a team of cricketing bikies got lost on the way and the fixture was cancelled. Wanganui is, you see, off the beaten track in every respect. It's a loose collection of timber houses set in the thick, wooded valleys around the Brunswick River, a few kilometres from the Heads and just south of the Queensland border.

It is a community of settlers, beatniks, farmers, writers – a mixture of the intrepid and the flotsam and jetsam of orderly life.

Everyone turned up, even the local transsexual. Older settlers wore older clothes, recalling the first residents – cedar-cutters who'd hacked their way through the scrub 130 years ago. When cedar ran out, they stayed because the climate was sub-tropical and the soil rich and volcanic. Banana and sugar crops were planted, and dwellers grew coffee, nuts, mangoes, grapefruit, limes and every imaginable vegetable.

Fishermen arrived and caught prawns, oysters, snapper and flounder. Surfers found a vigorous sea. Hippies smoked Mullumbimby Madness, a weed favoured in the 1960s. Religious cults found privacy. People were helped and respected. A bikie who'd lost a leg became a potter. A child of thalidomide built a recording studio. Everyone fought snakes and pests.

Cricket is the only game played in the area. Every valley has its team. In Wanganui they began playing four years ago in a field full of cattle and mushrooms. Being of the magic variety the mushrooms added to the entertainment. The locals were long-haired and a little out of it but they enjoyed themselves and so arranged games with neighbouring clusters of people. At first it was social cricket. They didn't play teams from the big smoke, Mullumbimby (pop 2,000), because they were too serious. They argued with umpires, things like that.

Wanganui is expressive of character and proud of its sense of time and space, and these virtues are captured in cricket. A bloke can do his own thing and yet must do his bit for others. And there's plenty of time for a beer and a chat.

Now they have their own field, and a majestic field it is, which a local dairy farmer offered to them a year ago. It was a cow paddock deep in the valley, sitting under towering hills of palm, gum, and camphor and with a creek running beside it. At first it was scrubby and the shape of an upturned bowl but the locals worked on it, driving tractors and digging and gradually they are flattening it. They've laid a concrete pitch in the middle and when the ground is completed it'll be one of the loveliest in the world.

Rather contrary to their instincts, they've begun practising twice a week. Games have been arranged every fortnight. Soon they'll play Brunswick. Pretty keen this Brunswick lot. Apparently they've already raised their eleven.

But today is Pioneer Day, a day for family, kids, oldtimers and laughter. They had shingle-splitting, gumboot throwing, candle making, tug-of-war and cross sawing (at which the *Herald* did not disgrace itself). When it rained the congregation sheltered under a canopy and sang songs of the 60s. Bush tucker was eaten and beer drunk.

Finally it was time for the twilight cricket. Upon being appointed umpire, I inquired of the rules and was referred to a bloke called Rafferty. Everyone was to have a go.

By and large the batting wasn't bad, if a shade on the bold side. Several sixes were hit though not nearly so many as were attempted. Mungo, fielding at deep cover, had so untroubled an afternoon that his defection to the beer tent was not noticed. Bowlers marked their runs with their straw hats and one removed his shirt.

A composition ball was used but occasionally it disappeared into the creek and someone would paddle in to fetch it. Longstop was an important position. Fielders took swigs of beer and barracked the batsmen. Upon Tony blocking a couple they shouted 'Is it a five-day game?' Tony pointed out that with 16 men fielding he was finding it difficult to penetrate. One fieldsman said that this failing had been widely reported, whereupon Tony reminded his audience of his four children. It was an evening of drink, sledging and humour. I can't say for certain which pair of batsmen were victorious, Mr Rafferty being inconclusive on the matter.

But these fellows will be enjoying their cricket whatever happens in Perth. Here the game is spreading because this plant does not depend upon its blossom.

CHARGING AT WINDMILLS

By all accounts, the Dutchman Carl Rackemann was only moderately gruntled to read that, like a porcelain teapot, he was good at his job but rather prone to breakages.

This bonehead Roebuck, he reckoned, might know something about English cricket but knew as much about its Australian cousin as he did about cane toads.

Now it is my turn to feel deeply hurt.

Brushing tears aside I must report that never, never before has anyone accused me of knowing anything about English cricket.

As friends have kindly, if a trifle persistently, pointed out it was I who led England's first and disastrous sortie to Amsterdam in which, setting out as pioneers, we returned as red-faced as strawberries in season.

It is time to tell the tale of this ill-fated trip, charging at windmills as someone called it.

Now, fair's fair, clear from your mind all images of Dutchmen walking out to bat in clogs and yodelling to their loved ones.

Apart from denying a bloke a fair go, such a picture betrays vagueness about Europe which is best kept hidden. For years our Dutch friends have played the game seriously and well.

Decades ago a far-sighted eccentric bought some marshland near Amsterdam and, being a sound fellow, converted it into cricket pitches.

The game took root and now the Netherlands has two indoor schools and a strong national league in which Test players, past and present, including Rohan Kanhai, Jack Richards and Rod McCurdy, have served as professionals.

Growing stronger, the Netherlands trounced the MCC last year, Cees Reeskins scoring 117 not out, and in 1990 they will host the mini-World Cup in which they expect to beat Zimbabwe.

The Tulip Tests had been arranged for August and, of course, a vast media party, scenting a story, accompanied the team.

I was appointed captain.

Apparently every other candidate was engaged elsewhere so a certain Mr Clayton summoned yours truly.

After a dawn flight, play began in Wuthering Heights weather at 2pm. Within minutes rain was pouring down. You see, it works even in benighted Europe.

An hour's play was lost and enquiries elicited the information that no overs were to be deducted from the 40. Condemned to bat in the gloom we concluded that Mr Rafferty had written the rules.

It was when Mr Nobby Clarke, who'd scored 150 for his island against England in 1973–74, smote Greg Thomas over his head and into a conveniently located dyke, that we began to think it might be an interesting afternoon.

An old codger fished out a muddy black pudding, swearing it was related to the red object which had recently descended in that region, whereupon it emerged that it is not done in the Netherlands to change a ball.

Thanks to Mr Clarke's combination of trenchant blocks and lofty blows, and thanks to staunch support from Lubbers and crew, the Netherlands made 177.

Like all pitches in the Netherlands, this one was artificial. Upon asking a local if he preferred real or artificial grass one local said he couldn't tell as he'd never smoked the latter.

Relying on dud info we had pitched the ball up, little knowing that in the Netherlands a half-vollë is a brand of milk, not a delivery.

And so it proved as the Dutch fast bowlers banged the ball down with passion and accuracy. Nevertheless, after 30 overs we were 1-115 and apparently in command.

Nothing is offered for guessing who was out.

Yet the cricket had been tightly contested and the Netherlands were playing out of their skins.

Then, like a blanket dropped on your head, night fell.

Suddenly we were scratching around and they were hot, catching and stopping everything. Batsmen were not watching the ball so much as looking for it while the fieldsmen seemed to have laser eyes.

Wickets fell and runs ran dry as the Netherlands, inspired by a partisan crowd, hustled and bustled. Nothing could save

England, no-one could find a soaring six or an edged boundary and we lost by five runs.

Of course we copped a bagging in the media who said it was a day of shame. Maybe they were right. Certainly my team was devastated. Yet it fought back to win by 90 runs the next day. More likely it was a freak in which the Netherlands, playing extremely well and riding their luck, beat a team which did not disgrace itself.

Frankly, this was as happy a time as any in my cricketing career for their hospitality and our spirits were superb.

Into each life a little rain must fall. And, anyhow, nothing is new. The Netherlands had beaten a Test country once before, in 1964. Their victims? Bobby Simpson's Australians!

THE TEAM FOR VENUS

Conclusive evidence has arrived at last to confirm a long-held suspicion that cricket is played on Venus. Astronauts dispatched to investigate the matter did not, it is true, actually see a game in progress but they took pictures of thunder and lightning and that is good enough for me.

No doubt our friends on Venus (who, hopefully, will have both arms intact) will be sorry to find out that cricket is no longer played in England but delighted to hear of its survival elsewhere. Beyond argument, an invitation will soon arrive from the Venus Board of Control (they will have one, depend upon it) challenging Earth to a Test match.

Accordingly, it is time to contemplate raising a team capable of boldly going where no team has gone before.

Now, picking a squad to tour New Zealand is a tricky enough operation and, frankly, Venus is even worse. For a start we cannot predict what their pitches will be like: apparently it hasn't rained on Venus for 280 million years, so they may resemble the wickets found in England last year. On the other hand, a thick atmosphere prevails which may offer swing, though temperatures are hotter even than those experienced in Adelaide. So hot in fact that zinc cream will be useless because zinc melts on Venus.

Despite these snippets of information we are shooting in the dark. We cannot foretell which leg before rule they use, nor when the second new ball may be taken. Heavens, we don't even know how many heads they have. All we can do is to pick our strongest XI and say our prayers. Naturally, Venus will ask your correspondent to select Earth's team (which is either very complimentary or extremely rude).

My opening batsmen will be Mark Taylor, that cheerful version of John Edrich, and Desmond Haynes, who was narrowly preferred to South African Jimmy Cook, an efficient opener skilful enough on the back foot to cope with craters.

At first drop it is a choice between Graeme Hick, who I believe will be dominant in the 1990s, and Martin Crowe. Since this inaugural Test is no place for beginners I will plump for Crowe. No matter what the computer ratings say, neither Richie Richardson nor Dilip Vengsarkar was a serious contender.

Javed Miandad is a shoo-in at four though we may need to bring Elastoplast for his mouth because with all those heads the local population may speak fluent Urdu and, accordingly, take offence. Our trip must be diplomatic for we are poorly placed for warfare.

Controversy may accompany my preference for Allan Border as captain and pillar of the middle order in front of Viv Richards and Dean Jones. Border has made runs on all pitches and against every variety of bowling, and has led with fortitude. A visit to Venus where he has never made a hundred might freshen his spirit and if we are in trouble there is no man I'd rather see marching out.

Distinguished and dazzling Jeffrey Dujon must play at six to be followed by an allrounder, a more difficult choice.

Ian Botham appears to be in decline, Imran's bowling lacks sting, Steve Waugh isn't bowling at all and Kapil Dev's form has been scratchy. West Indian Franklyn Stephenson, purveyor of a wicked slower ball and an energetic batsman to boot, a gifted enough cricketer to do the double in county cricket two years ago, is a strong contender but I will opt for Richard Hadlee despite his recent injury. Hadlee is a risk. Fully fit of course his selection would be automatic.

Malcolm Marshall and Wasim Akram, champions of different decades, bowlers of versatility, persistence and intelligence, will play at eight and nine while, despite everything, Abdul Qadir is the only possible choice as spinner. Inhabitants of Venus may have solved the riddle of the infinite but I defy them to pick Qadir's googly.

Volatile and outlandish he may be, and perhaps the last of a dying breed too; nevertheless Qadir is far ahead of proven rivals around the world. One place remains to be filled and we may as well choose another bowler. Ambrose is liable to fade, Patterson is inconsistent and while South African Allan Donald is incisive he is also untested in these circles.

Terry Alderman, as clever a bowler as was ever born, merits selection and yet I fancy we need someone young and strong to complete our side.

Raw as he is, I will choose Ian Bishop who may emerge beside Akram and Hick as great cricketers of the next decade. So there it is: Taylor, Haynes, Crowe, Javed, Border, Dujon, Akram, Hadlee, Marshall, Qadir and Bishop.

A Test on Venus will not last five days, but if it did a result would be certain no matter how dilatory the overrate. A day on Venus lasts 224 Earth days so we must construct the rules carefully. Merv Hughes will serve as 12th man and no manager will be appointed. Our team will leave next month provided the astronauts are not on strike.

A Precarious
Preoccupation

Pre-Season Training

THIS morning, Skipper Rose appointed Popplewell in charge of training. I announced that this was the most disastrous appointment ever. Popplewell is a fitness fanatic. We'll be hunting across wetlands, through hidden lanes, doing press-ups in sheds and sprinting in farmyards and all the while Nigel will be swearing at us. He only swears because all trainers swear and because he suspects that some of us wouldn't run fast unless someone was swearing.

As a matter of fact, I didn't run too badly today. Sixth out of, oh, twelve at least. Wasn't so good at the piggy-back races, though. The relation between piggy-backs and fending off Imran Khan was a little too remote for me to grasp.

Practice

Shortly after my return to work this morning I sustained a blow on my finger from a lifter in the indoor nets bowled by G. Palmer. I developed a large blood blister. It's been a lovely start to the season.

Moreover I batted poorly. As usual, my drives all screwed through square leg like some hack golfer. Put a bloke there and I'm out of business.

To add to my sense of horror, I saw a sheet which listed my last season's dismissals. Apparently I was bowled a mere five times, lbw only four times, stumped twice and caught 36 times! 36!! If I hit the ball on the ground, they'd never get me out.

Most of those catches were from shots aimed through point. My bat twists either too far or not far enough when I play that shot. I've never been very good at it (there was a shed in the covers in my back yard at home and no runs were available that way). In the past I've not tried to play that shot much. If I stick to the shots I'm good at, I'll score more runs. Trouble is, all the other teams know exactly which shots I'm good at, and they bowl a good length on off stump to me. I must find an answer.

With quickies, I simply have to leave the ball alone and, if they are happy wasting the new ball, so be it. With spinners it's more difficult. If I avoid trying to hit the ball through cover point, what shall I do with it? Can't just ignore it. By the time the spinners are on I ought to be trying to dominate. I'll just have to attack them. Ken McEwan, who has a reputation as a prodigious hitter of spinners, says he only started clobbering slow bowlers because he didn't think he could play them normally.

Team Meeting

Botham has called a meeting for this evening at 9.45 to discuss the game. Our meetings have never made a scrap of difference before. We don't so much prepare as arrive. I think our attitude is 'Let the opposition worry about us, we don't want to know anything at all about them.' Analysis can do harm sometimes. Before last season's Benson & Hedges Final I asked Garner what Hadlee bowled, as I'd never faced him, and he replied, 'He's as quick as me and moves the ball both ways!'

Getting to the Ground

We plod along, desperate to reach the blessed relief of the motorway as soon as possible – so many fewer decisions to make on motorways, less concentration required of tired brains. Richard, Vic and I settle down for the journey. I switch on the radio, listen to the World Service or Radio 4, anything to avoid the monotony of the Test match in which Boycott and Tavaré are fighting a noble rearguard action. We follow a drama about an artist, a tortured genius (I ask Vic if he is a tortured genius and he replies, 'Only when they sweep my arm ball'), who eventually is successful. Immediately he commits suicide. Apparently his devoted wife had painted his famous portraits and he was ashamed to admit it.

Tension Mounts

Before the game I was incredibly nervous. It was ridiculous to be so tense on such a sunlit day at such a lovely ground. Yet I was almost sick with worry. I had a headache before the toss, I was edgy with trying to work out how to bat against Hadlee on a flyer. Really, it's only cricket, it's stupid to fret so much.

As it turned out we were in the field without a chance of batting and there was nothing to worry about. I spent the afternoon in the slips, chatting to Botham and Marks, mostly about what sort of egg it was best to have for breakfast. Of course we did concentrate hard when the bowler was bowling, but cricket is played 6½ hours a day for 105 days out of 125 and it's vital to drift away between balls and between days.

Early Dismissal

Out first ball! Can you believe it? A month of cross-country runs, 2000 balls on a bloody ball machine and I'm out first ball. It's outrageous.

My indignation has been slightly assuaged by beer, as it is 10 pm as I write and we've spent most of the evening driving towards Trent Bridge for tomorrow's game. We stopped in a pub along the way for steak and kidney pie. And anyway the whole thing was so preposterous that even I could see a faintly amusing side to it.

My first ball of the 1983 season was bowled by a gentleman of Oxford called Varey, who has established something of a reputation of a batsman but none at all as a bowler. It was a wet pitch and I'd planned to play back but, watching Varey's hiccupping run-up, decided that I could safely push forward. As the ball came towards me I plunged out. The ball pitched on a length, rose amiably and touched my glove before lolloping to the wicket-keeper. I walked as soon as I felt the touch, not because I am a walker – walkers are a sanctimonious shower – but because there didn't seem much point in hanging around looking desperate. I gather the sound of leather on willow has pleased the poets. I can report that the sound of leather on glove is not remotely romantic.

Reactions

After I was out I sat in the dressing room, watching my team-mates react to their dismissals. Whether he scores 100 or 0, Denning sits down, unstraps his pads and lights a cigar.

Popplewell is usually furious, especially if he's been out to a defensive shot which frustrates his battling personality. Richards can be stormy, causing a hasty abandonment of the room, or he can be silent with a hint of dozing annoyance. Botham usually laughs as if it matters not. He never regrets anything he's done. Today Marks and Dredge were both in high dudgeon that they'd lost their wickets to tame catches at short leg. Both would rather have been out in some more valiant way. Our second innings should be interesting.

Technical Considerations

I must try to iron out my weaknesses before May (if you could see my ironing you would think my choice of verb unfortunate). In cricket you have to try always to move either to the line of the ball or according to its length. Most opening batsmen choose their shot depending upon the line of the ball in relation to the stumps. Men like Edrich, Lawry, Boycott leave alone as many balls as possible early in their innings.

On the other hand, most middle-order batsmen want to hit the ball. They let far fewer deliveries pass, they want to dominate the bowlers. Their stroke is determined by the length of the ball. Can they drive or pull? If not, they may settle for defence. The line of the ball is much less relevant, and wide long-hops are not wasted.

Rain

The rain started at 2 a.m. this morning and it hasn't stopped yet. Trent Bridge is smothered with puddles. We'll not play tomorrow. And so I enter May without having scored a run yet. So far I've been paid about £1200 this season. I caught two catches at Oxford and didn't bowl, which means I'm on about £600 a catch – rather more, I think, than baseball players.

Cricketers' Association

I spent most of the day in Birmingham, attending our Cricketers' Association meeting. John Arlott is our President and has taken to making superbly crusty speeches, a sort of wined Solzhenitsyn of cricket. Under his guidance our debates are always fair, with each speech heard in silence, however outrageous (and Boycott has spoken).

Before lunch we had a rather solemn debate about the state of English cricket. Everyone seems worried about the state of English everything. No-one knew what to do about it, or at least everyone knew what to do but no-one could agree on anything. Four-day cricket? Leagues? Fewer overseas players? Better pitches?

Botham's Horse Races

We had an excellent morning spent playing Botham's game of horse races with new rules developed by Roebuck. We put two jokers in the pack and announced that every time a joker came out, the horses in the lead fell. With any luck we could cut out two or three joint leaders when the joker emerged, which meant that anyone backing those suits lost. This caused much wild excitement and no little profit. Actually the room was filled with hysterical shouts as men roared 'Come on, spades', 'Get on, my boy', 'What the hell's clubs' jockey doing?', 'Get the whip out, man!' and so on. It really is a tremendous game which went on for two hours with Botham winning £25 and everyone extremely excited by the host of close finishes. It was emotional, you know, when you were on spades to win and they led all the way, only to be wiped out at the final fence by the appearance of the joker. All those roars, all those hoarse cheers to waste.

Mastery

The lovely thing about scoring a century is that it proves you're the master for the day. Somehow if you're out for 97 rather than 102, people hardly notice and even cricketers will say, 'He should have scored 100' as if those extra few runs make much difference. Unless you score 100 you haven't really asserted your mastery, the innings is not fully matured. Someone once said (he was an idiot) that batting, like life, consists of three stages: not birth, life and death but in, innings, out. If you reach 100 years of age, the Queen sends you a telegram; if you hit 100 runs, opponents congratulate you and headlines proclaim you.

I was out to the last ball of our innings for 105, caught off a swipe. I haven't scored a century for two years in first-class cricket and have passed 50 thirty times in between, so let me remember all I can about today's cricket.

For a start I batted in a floppy hat as I had last week. I don't think this makes any difference unless it helps relaxation. If you wear a helmet it's likely to put you on your guard as if you are expecting trouble, like wearing a holster in westerns, but then sometimes you are right. Apart from that there was nothing physically unusual in my approach today or in my feeling. I can't remember being unusually fluent or confident before the game. I felt as an actor must feel before every performance. A part of me was saying, 'Oh hell, I must go out there again' and a part of me was trying to create a mood which would reduce my chances of buggering the whole thing up.

Nor did I do anything technically different as far as I can see. At first I picked up my bat only a little as Lawrence was bowling fast and I hoped to guide them to third man. Sainsbury opened the bowling at the other end with his left-arm swingers and he bowled well, so I had to rely upon nicks and tucks to pick up some runs. Denning and Richards came and went. I think it was the dismissal of Richards that gave me my chance to play a long innings. No longer was I batting with a nagging doubt that Richards and Botham were to come, straining at the leash: Botham was already in and Richards out.

I reached 40 and quite frankly I still hadn't played any particularly notable shots. We were 100 for 2 in 22 overs, and by this time Botham had injured his leg and had a runner. Botham lashed out and was eventually caught for 73. I decided it was about time I started to go for my shots and lifted my bat shoulder-high. That was the only change in technique I observed through this innings. In the last ten overs I hit a few powerful straight drives which persuaded Graveney to drop long-on and long-off back. This was an important breakthrough since it meant I could get a single any time I wanted one. I late-cut Shepherd and he said that no-one had done that to him since Frank Worrell. Next ball I squeezed him from off stump to square leg and we laughed as if to say, 'Well, Frank Worrell wouldn't have done that.'

I did hit one good shot to a straight ball from Doughty. It was on a good length and I waited for it to reach me before dropping my bat and whipping it through mid-wicket to the boundary. 'Big Bird' Garner joined me for the last over and I was on 99.

He hit one to gully and said, 'Run.' If Romaines had hit the stumps I'd have been run out. Next ball I guided one for four to reach 100. It was a marvellous feeling and a relief to show people that I could go on with my innings when the time was right.

It's strange that I can't detect any significant difference in today's innings and any of the other 50 or 60 that I play every year. If I could, I might have more chance of repeating it.

Another Day

The facts. It's 6.15 p.m. and we're hanging on for dear life. Well, I am at any rate. Jerry Lloyds is smashing the ball all over the place. Mallender comes in to bowl. The ball is short of a length and outside the off stump. Roebuck plays back. The ball keeps low and nips into his pads and onto the middle stump.

The case for the prosecution. Why the hell did he play back? Didn't he see all day that the ball was keeping low? It's a typical Northampton pitch and however hard Mallender hammers them into it, they'll always keep low. So why did he play back? He was asking for trouble.

The case for the defence. I've scored 1150 runs batting like that this season. Am I to abandon that technique merely because the pitch is particularly slow?

Verdict. Yes, of course you are, you clot. There's a thousand runs in this pitch for any batsman who plays forward every ball. And you, a reasonably experienced, intelligent human being, played back in the first over.

Search for a Formula

I avoided the papers today as much as I could. They're bound to use some adjectives to describe my innings (except *The Times* – Alan Gibson writes for them and his train is usually late and so he misses my knock) and I don't want anyone else's judgements disturbing my own analysis. If they'd said I was studious I'd probably go and try to be studious tomorrow, hoping for a second good score. Their description would become my prescription, a solution in the never-ending search for a successful formula which might disrupt the fresh spirit that I must bring to each and every innings.

A Leg-Spinner Too

From the hotel I caught an underground train to the West End. Lunch in a café and then a stroll round Trafalgar Square, a burst of freedom, a place to roam where people and pigeons know nothing of cricket. Popped into the National Gallery because it happened to be there and at 2.30 off to the first of three plays I saw today. First *Pirates of Penzance* in Drury Lane – marvellous; are professional actors really as joyous as that or do they all hate each other? Next *The Real Thing* in which Tom Stoppard showed to a Scottish revolutionary that just as a lump of wood isn't necessarily a good cricket bat, so a string of words isn't necessarily good writing. Finally, after a pizza, to *Another Country* at Queens. I didn't escape from cricket in this play, either. Austin Mitchell used a school game as the background for his penultimate scene. His team included a Marxist, a homosexual, a liberal, a sadist and, although we didn't see the other seven, I expect there was a leg-spinner too.

Excuses

First bad decision of the season. It wasn't out, never. Lbw? How can you be lbw to a left-arm spinner on a turning pitch when your foot is down the pitch and probably outside off stump?

It was a moral decision. Umpires sometimes take it upon themselves to impose good batsmanship upon their charges much as moral re-armers hope to impose decency on society. I took it into my head to sweep across the line and umpires don't like that sort of thing. With some you never sweep because if you miss, you're dead. This fellow wasn't one of those but he raised a finger of condemnation anyway. If I'd been plodding forward in respectful manner I would have been safe, in fact the bowler wouldn't have bothered to appeal. I felt robbed of my wicket but surprisingly maintained a dignified silence even in the dressing room, though I did explain in a bemused voice that it couldn't have been out. Someone should write a book of cricket excuses.

Wind

What a remarkable difference wind makes to cricket. No wonder Boycott hangs out a handkerchief as he walks in to bat. Today the bowlers at one end were running into a gusty wind which pushed them off-balance and also helped the batsmen to drive. Even the fastest man bowling into the wind scarcely needed anyone behind square – the ball simply did not go there – whereas downwind bowlers needed most of their men behind square.

Marks and I first discovered the significance of wind when we were playing for Somerset against New Zealand years ago. A roly-poly man called McIntyre was bowling into the wind and Vic said that if anyone could hit the ball into the air it was bound to go for six. He said a spinner could hardly bowl into the wind at Taunton with short boundaries behind him. In went Vic to bat. To prove his point, he danced down the pitch to drive McIntyre up into the air. He missed the ball and was bowled. We didn't discuss the role of wind in cricket for some time after that.

Getting Out

God, how I hate getting out. I poked around again. Edged in a single somewhere and then had my off stump knocked back. It was a good ball, at least I think it was. I say it left me and kept low. My partner, Richards, says it kept low and nipped back. It was probably straight.

The Trough

Wandered around the back alleys of Northampton this evening, stopping for a hamburger in some basement café, and then sat on a wall outside the hotel watching the cars go by. Most of the fellows were in a pub – 'Bilko' Waight had announced that he intended to do something different this evening, and we'd supposed he'd bought tickets for the opera or something, but it turned out that rather than sitting in the hotel bar he was going to a pub up the road – but I wanted to collect my thoughts in solitude.

Almost every season I sink into a trough of despondency which lasts sometimes a week, sometimes a day. For some reason I seem unable to last from April to September without a bout of morose self-examination. I can sense a growing upheaval within and I'm afraid it will not easily be stilled.

It is inevitable, I suppose, that the trough usually occurs when my form is bad. It is strange that I am doing rather well at the moment and nevertheless feel disturbed. I batted with fortitude at Maidstone and scored 100 runs in the last match against Surrey. There's hardly been time to worry, and from a cricket point of view there is no sense at all in this turmoil.

And yet it is building. Worse, we have eight more days away from home, living on top of each other, sleeping in the same hotel rooms, travelling, playing, training, fielding and eating all together with scarcely any outside influence, as if we were a group of monks who eschewed the world and its people. There is going to be no escape from the rigours of our life on the road for one week. Most bad things that happen to a cricket team happen on away trips, when our lives are dominated by our ephemeral gifts. I can return home after a game at Taunton and put on a record, pick up a novel and not care a jot about events down the road. Away, it is on top of you all the time.

Well, tomorrow I must arise and go to Northampton's cricket ground, surrounded as it is by red-bricked terraced houses, dominated as it is by bleak, empty football stands.

A Right To-do

Today's match was rained off. A large crowd had gathered to enjoy the sunny weather but the outfield was saturated and at 1.45, without warning, the game was abandoned. Naturally, Somerset supporters who had driven 170 miles for the game were furious, and there was a right to-do in the pavilion, especially when the Surrey officials would not refund entrance money. Cricket is its own worst enemy at times.

A Fierce Dog

This morning I had a chat with Viv. In his different way he had been in an emotional cauldron these last few days, too. He was impressive, finding words and ideas to match his passion. He said sometimes people can be like a house with a fierce dog outside. Do you go into a house with a fierce dog outside? No, so how can these people expect anyone to help them? He said it wasn't a matter of cricket, there is no sense in blaming cricket, it is what people do to themselves that causes their turmoil.

We talked for an hour and a half. I've never known Richards

more convincing and yet even at the end of the conversation, I still could see no sense in persevering. It still seemed ridiculous to carry on banging one's head. It still seemed a worthless exist-ence, an empty experiment with a character which did nothing for team-mates and ignored the acres of ability which could con-tribute something more constructive.

It occurred to me that if Viv could not talk me around, no-one could, myself apart. And so before lunch I went for a stroll around the ground with Vic Marks. Upon reflection, this is when a light began to appear. We sat on a bench on the far side of the ground and laughed about things. Vic was supposed to be convincing me that one must persevere. As it was, my competitive instincts were aroused and I won the debate. We concluded that it would be a jolly good idea to pack in cricket. We laughed at this dis-covery; we'd rather hoped to reach the opposite view. We agreed that not only should I retire but he should, too!

Humour returned after this. It wasn't so much strength and self-respect that fortified me but rather a realisation that what I had lacked had been the sardonic sense of humour which offers a shield against the severest blows.

Home

10.15, nearly home, time for food. We escape into a pub for a mixed grill and a pint of best. Thank heaven for motorways – tediously predictable, but what must it have been like before them? How could WG have played cricket after a long journey in a carriage with little suspension? We bubble cheerfully on for the last few miles which somehow or other seem to take ages. As the marathon runners say, 'It's not the 26 miles that hurt, it's the 286 yards at the end.' Eventually, though, another journey is completed, we can put our feet up at home, unpack our suit-cases and sleep in our own beds.

Fear of Failure

Our scorer has presented us with our statistics of the season. I avoided being caught quite so often, only 28 times compared to 36. On the other hand I've been bowled 12 times, run out 3 and lbw 7 times (according to the umpires at any rate) and stumped only once. Apparently I batted for 1920 more minutes than anyone else in county games and scored more slowly than anyone else except Richard Ollis.

If I dared to risk being stumped more often, perhaps I would be more entertaining. After all, I went down the pitch lots of times and missed only once. It's a good risk. Perhaps, though, it's not in my nature. I was spurred on by fear of dismissal and fear of failure. These affect my conduct much more than any joy in hitting the ball or any love of success.

SOME QUICK MEN

THE LONG BLACK
TELEGRAPH POLE

A COUPLE of nights before our 1979 Gillette Cup semi-final the Somerset players were entertained by one of our most devoted supporters, John Cleese. During the brief interludes when the players managed to escape the attentions of dead parrots, John Cleese was to be seen in deep and profound conversation with Joel Garner. This provoked a most diverting thought – could this be a new comedy team developing? Certainly both men have remarkable limbs, including several arms and legs each acting independently of all others. Perhaps they might start with a guest appearance on *Come Dancing*, offering a fresh approach to the Tango. Anyhow, let the Muppets beware.

John Cleese's comic abilities are well known and at least partly unconscious; Dennis Breakwell could scarcely control himself when Cleese attempted to pour him some wine. Perhaps the cork should have been removed first! That Joel Garner is a figure of similar hilarity is less well known. Indeed, most opposing batsmen seem quite unable to appreciate his talents: the somewhat improbable cohesion of Big Bird's arms and legs as he flaps in to bowl provokes not one whit of joy in these dour opponents. Not that they ignore him entirely. The more long-in-the-chewing-gum among them will greet Joel with a cheerful 'Good morning' and will add a sympathetic if trifle optimistic, 'A bit chilly for fast bowling, isn't it?' But apart from such pleasantries, few appreciate the range of Garner's talents.

Of course, there are good reasons for this widespread ignorance. For a start, it is almost impossible to understand anything Joel says. He talks in a strange lingo, presumably a broad Barbadian banter, which shares no words (so far as one can tell) with the mother tongue as she is spoken from Chewton Mendip to Nether Stowey. Consequently, conversation with Joel tends to be a hazardous business. Ask him for the time and his reply might vary from the earthy 'In the car park' to the wholly mystical 'Well, I haven't been there for a while'.

Naturally, being a fast bowler, Big Bird can afford to be a little elusive. He need only say a few words and follow with a great laugh for the whole dressing room to be in uproar. And when he pops into the visitors' room for a little social chit-chat, he enjoys a marvellously attentive audience. The room practically falls apart at the slightest hint of a witticism. Fast bowlers are treated with the most touching affection.

Big Bird rather likes being so very black, so very large and so very difficult to decipher. He feels no obligation to hide his considerable light under a nearby bushel (not that they make bushels like that nowadays) like some reluctant débutante (and where have they all gone?). He fairly relishes using his long reach to best advantage in a darts game, placing rather than propelling his darts into the board. After a particularly successful day he will stroll around the main streets of Taunton with the whites of his eyes and gleaming teeth visible for miles around, thoroughly pleased with the glances of astonished children and terrified babies. Or, if there's a bit of a crowd in, Joel will charge around the boundary with kangaroo strides, pick up the ball in one gigantic hand and hurl it as far as possible in the general direction of the stumps. If, perchance, wicket-keeper Derek Taylor is the correct distance away, the ball will land with a thud in his gloves. If not, well at least the crowd will appreciate the spectacle of the throw and the sight of fielders diving around, some trying to stop the ball, others desperate to avoid its perilous trajectory.

This slightly mischievous use of his powers sometimes extends to Joel's batting. As with most fast bowlers, Big Bird is immensely impressed by his own style. Often he talks of his desire to 'flick' the ball here and to 'lick' it there. Occasionally the most ambitious strokes succeed gloriously, for instance when Les Taylor was dispatched for a powerful straight six at Leicester as Joel tried to coax victory from defeat. Even if success eludes him, Joel is well worth watching at the crease, particularly when in tandem with Derek Taylor. Derek runs in very short, scampered steps which contrast dramatically with Big Bird's massive strides and frequently leave him in danger of being lapped.

Actually Joel's batting has developed these past two years. No longer do we ponder upon his ability to lift the ball very high but not very far. The nine iron has been abandoned for the wood, and Joel lashes the ball very hard and very straight these days. Some of his strokes 'on the up' at Bath in 1981 were worthy of the master himself, and neither the master nor the rest of us any longer doubt Big Bird when he announces his intention to smite 50 in 10 overs.

Not that Joel is an exuberant West Indian fast bowler every day. Cheerful times are interspersed with periods of reflective silence during which Joel retires behind one of the thrillers he reads so voraciously (or *The Gulag Archipelago* if the mood is really grim). If these gloomy thoughts do surface it is usually to express frustration at authorities who govern without sensitivity. Joel has an astute, lively mind and can be angered by thoughtless administrators who make demands that he feels to be unfair. Big Bird is a thorough professional who does his job as well as he is able, which is very well, and he does not appreciate interference from amateurs. It is, perhaps, just as well that he is discreet, for Joel is not one to bed down early at the beckoning of selectors or chairmen. Before Somerset's 1979 Gillette Cup victory Joel was in a night club, quietly drinking and chatting until the early hours of the morning. He knew he would not sleep if he obeyed the curfew, and realised he would perform much better if he slept for six hours rather than tossing and turning for nine.

Joel does have an independent, self-reliant nature. He designed and built his own villa in Barbados and then brought off a remarkable coup by immediately renting it at a high fee to American bankers. Big Bird's anger at authorities is surprising in many ways. He has repeatedly shown himself to have a cool, detached temperament. He responds with neither words nor gestures to the most provocative attack by opponent or spectator. Should a fast bowler be so sadly misled as to whistle a bouncer past Joel's ears (no mean feat in itself), Big Bird will merely smile benevolently down the pitch as if to say (as might the frog to the tadpole), 'Your turn will come'. Another Somerset bowler has been known, in similar circumstances, to inform the ill-advised bowler, 'if you had another brain cell, you'd be a plant' – but that's not Joel's style.

Nor does Joel permit himself the luxury of being upset by crowds. At Harrogate a supporter addressed some unpleasant remarks to Big Bird as he lolloped out to bat (just when, as chance would have it, the groundsman was warming up the heavy roller). Rather than give any indication that he had so much as heard these remarks, let alone been hurt or angered by them, Joel proceeded to bat with aplomb, contributing a flamboyant 53 before bowling some distinctly hasty overs to Boycott and Lumb.

So despite his keen intelligence, Joel is far too full of fun to be irritated for long. He prefers to quieten raucous spectators by performance rather than repartee. He bears no malice, though he lies in wait for a couple of people who did him wrongs years ago. Lancashire rejected him in 1978 and one of their players reported, 'Garner can't bowl'. That man has not scored too many runs against Somerset since!

In fact Joel is so cool, so dispassionate, that his colleagues try to steam him up by passing on supposedly overheard comments. Viv Richards once whispered to Joel that he'd heard Alan Ealham say, 'Garner isn't fast, though he does obtain steep bounce'. Read about the Somerset v. Kent game in 1979 to see the damaging results! We'll never know if Ealham ever said anything of the sort, of course.

It is easy to underestimate Joel. His talents are wide-ranging. As he lives two houses down from me, I've learned to appreciate his cooking, his delicate typing, the scope of his reading, his hospitality (as Clyde Walcott said, 'Richards is king of the cricket, but Garner is king of the night!') and his mowing (quite a sight!).

It is just as easy, and far more deadly, to under-rate his bowling. His run-up is short and his delivery deceptively effortless. But no colleague or opponent of Joel will deny that he is one of the very fastest bowlers in the world. Certainly he is one of the most awkward, hammering the ball into the grass from a height far above sight-screens which were built with less prodigious mortals in mind. Joel generates remarkable bounce from apparently docile pitches and has the ability to change pace without any noticeable change of action. With these abilities it is not easy to decide whether Joel most resembles Jeff Thomson or Tom Cartwright. Like Thomson, he is capable of bouncing the ball from a good length into the batsman's ribs and of maintaining a menacing hostility on slow pitches. And, like Cartwright, he can produce controlled movement in either direction (not at the same time, unless bemused victims are to be believed, but often in the same delivery) without sacrificing line and length.

Perhaps the truth is that Big Bird will bowl like Cartwright when the mood so takes him and like Thomson if he feels sharp and aggressive. In the West Indies team, Joel is usually used as a stock bowler to hold the fort while Roberts, Holding, Daniel, Marshall et al are resting: it may be that this use of Joel is founded on a shrewd appreciation of his nature, with his relatively mild temperament and whole-hearted dislike of conceding runs.

As a defensive bowler Joel is well-nigh supreme. Few others could bowl at the end of a thriving Sunday League innings to Allan Lamb and Peter Willey with seven men in behind the bat. Nor are many bowlers of his pace as willing to bowl long spells for their team – not many fast bowlers would have volunteered to bowl all afternoon and evening one hot Harrogate day to save their side from defeat. It is never difficult to persuade Big B to bowl but sometimes it can be hard to stop him.

No doubt Joel will play cricket for only a few years more. He enjoys himself in Taunton but longs for a leisurely life on the beaches of Barbados with the friends from his days of poverty. He vows never to return to the huts and rags of his youth, and with his shrewd business sense he never will. But until he retires, the 'long black telegraph pole' will continue to grace the cricket fields of the world with his disciplined bowling, his flamboyant strokeplay and his wide, cheerful smile.

HADLEE THE LEAN MACHINE

It's hard to say whether a batsman about to face Richard Hadlee feels more like a patient in a dentist's chair who is beginning to regret his penchant for chocolate, or a pupil in a headmaster's study who's ruing his fondness for cigarettes.

Hadlee makes batsmen aware of their faults by constantly probing them. Not too good against outswingers, eh? Well, here is one. And here's another. The batsman hangs in there, dreading every delivery, watching for the sneaky one that breaks back into him.

To take guard with Hadlee at the top of his mark, you must have a stout heart and a secure technique. It isn't that Hadlee is fast – only occasional deliveries are quick enough to brush your moustache – simply that he is so good.

He intimidates with movement, to counter which batsmen pessimistically reduce their backlifts. Anyhow, he bowls so few bad balls, and there's no point in dreaming. Not one of his 458 deliveries for New Zealand in the third Test against Australia at the MCG last week was hooked, and barely one hit to leg.

And his run-up is so innocuous! If he's going to be demonic, he might at least charge in from somewhere over the rainbow. From a dozen measured paces he can move the ball either way, and vary his pace wickedly. Really, it isn't fair.

His repertoire includes a fierce bumper that rears past your chin – Allan Border was nearly decapitated by one in Melbourne. He has, too, a slower ball which he holds back in his wrist at delivery. This is the masterpiece in his collection. Dean Jones fell for it after he'd been softened up with a couple of leg-cutters, and even Border had a swish at one. It's as elusive as Qadir's googly.

Facing Hadlee, a batsman has all these things on his mind. Still, there may be good times just around the corner. He might be taken off. It's not as if the blessed bloke ever says anything. Hadlee can be pictured, silent and brooding, emerging from the mist in one of those Boris Karloff movies. It's all part of the effect. Hadlee isn't snooty really, but he understands his own game and realises that it pays him to bowl with a cold heart. Ian Botham may turn games into jousts, may buy wickets when he's stuck. Hadlee disdains such loose living, and is quietly menacing as he goes about his work.

He lost his temper with Botham 10 years ago, rising to a bait and bowling a bombardment of bouncers which cost his team dearly. He doesn't go in for that sort of thing these days, doesn't need to. Why would he when he has so many different types of delivery at his command, and 373 Test wickets – level with Botham's record – in the bag to prove it?

Hadlee is the best bowler in the world, and has been for five years. He knows it, and so do the batsmen. As he stands ready to bowl, you wonder which of those deliveries he's selected for you.

Hadlee is formidable because he's disciplined. His run-up and action are as grooved as a clock, so that he gives nothing away, pinning the batsman down as he works him over. He tries one ball. If you survive it, he flicks his eyebrows, hitches his trousers and strides back to his mark to continue to ask a hundred questions.

He is already superbly skilled, and despite his 36 years and spindly body he appears to be getting better. His greatness stems from a decision he made a few years ago to change from a teara-way into an economical bowler dependent on movement and variety. He'd never been as good a fast bowler as Dennis Lillee, and now he was too old for all that charging about. So he cut down his run. Stubbornly ignoring critics, he concentrated on bowling wicket to wicket. Running in so close to the stumps that people were amazed he didn't clatter into them, and with his arm rigidly at 12 o'clock, Hadlee metamorphosed into a bowler with a wide range of deliveries who was quick enough to push batsmen back. Wickets began to tumble. By accident, almost, he'd hit on his route to greatness.

At the MCG last week he took 10 wickets in a Test for the eighth time, moving past Barnes, Grimmett and Lillee. Of his victims, six were leg-before and four caught in the slip region. All were batsmen, every one of whom protected his wicket with spirit. Hadlee doesn't take fortuitous wickets. He planned the downfall of those eight batsmen, and executed those plans. On a fair pitch he took 10 for 176 in 75 overs of majestic bowling.

He is the master of a genre that requires concentration and analysis, a writer of detective fiction, not Victorian romps.

In Brisbane two years ago he gave the performance of a lifetime, or so it appeared. It wasn't. He's always good, but last week he was remarkable. He even chuckled occasionally, if somewhat chillingly. He'll be missed in England next season. We need someone to expose our bad habits. Chocolate and cigarettes aren't good for you, are they?

WASIM AKRAM

Begging forgiveness of Sir Richard and Mr Marshall, it has to be said that Wasim Akram, of Lahore and Lancashire, is currently the hottest property in cricket. Every time he removes his sweater a buzz rushes around the ground like a bush fire across parched land. It is a sense of something about to happen. Wasim shares with Marshall an air of unleashed athleticism.

Within 12 months Wasim has scored a scorching Test hundred in Adelaide, rescuing his team, and worked such wonders with the ball as to win comparison with Alan Davidson – the highest of compliments. To round it off, he has just won a cup for his county with two searing bursts, one in Manchester and one at Lord's. Last Saturday he gave Worcestershire a fearful shaking. Curtis was beaten for pace, Hick shocked by a bumper and Botham driven backwards as Wasim nailed his men. On Wednesday these fellows asked Jimmy Cook how Wasim might best be played. 'From the bowler's end,' was the reply.

Somerset had found his bowling in the semi-final just as awesome, their steady ascendance being interrupted by a whirlwind that created chaos where once there had been order.

At Lord's, Wasim to Hick was to be the key. At Manchester, it was Cook who stood between Lancashire and victory. Bowling with terrific pace, nearly decapitating his chosen victim, Wasim beat Cook time and again, sapping morale in ranks used to seeing Cook in control.

Because Wasim's arm is so fast in revolution, batsmen find it difficult to judge his length, and find themselves playing back when safety insists upon pushing forward. Like Marshall, his short deliveries climb cruelly, while those of fuller length surprise with skid. Perhaps he lacks Marshall's astonishing ability to sustain an assault, and possibly his durability as well, but he is the better man in limited-overs cricket and at mopping up a tail.

Wasim was hardly less resistible in Australia, making the ball not so much talk as swear. Hustling in off a short run, flashing his arm over, he challenged every batsman with deliveries which spat off the pitch. In Melbourne and in Adelaide he revealed a range of skills far beyond most bowlers, ancient or modern. Wasim has a bouncer so fast that Viv Richards, paying unique respect, will not hook at it. Hick's face, upon encountering this delivery, bore eloquent testimony to its danger. Wasim also has the best yorker since Joel Garner gave his boots to the Navy. And, gentle reader, it is the truth, Wasim can swing the ball both ways.

By and large his short deliveries move away, by and large those of full length cut back. But these rules are frequently honoured in the breach. Swinging the old ball as much as the new, he is no less of a threat in mid-afternoon than early morning. Intimidating with movement as much as terror, whenever he bowls a tumble of wickets appears probable.

Alarmingly, Wasim has one more skill, one he executes with magical precision. He can bowl round and over the wicket with equal facility. From around, his yorkers explode into the stumps, as if fired from wide mid-off.

It is a bagful of tricks. Moreover, Wasim is an analytical bowler. No Australian batsman escaped easily from his clutches last winter. Wasim haunted Steve Waugh with in-swingers, and harassed Dean Jones with deliveries climbing from a length.

To Mark Taylor, so unmemorable of feature, so stoical of temperament, he simply bowled one magnificent delivery after another, most of which Taylor survived, few of which he mastered. It was a virtuoso display from Wasim.

His hundred in Adelaide was hardly less meritorious. Joining Imran in a dark hour, he struck rousing off-drives to push Australia back. Hitherto, his batting had been lightweight, his arms and his mind cherishing their freedom too much. With this effort he showed the fighting spirit, if not yet the stature, of a Botham. He bats, sometimes, like a colt not yet broken. Nevertheless this is an invigorating, fervent cricketer, a player capable of turning any match. He has the dedication, as well as the talent, to answer the clarion call of greatness.

After collecting his gold medal last weekend he went, not to Stringfellows, but to bed, to prepare for his Sunday League game. And it took hours of practice to master that toe-crushing yorker.

Can it last? Plainly, Wasim could be cricket's most exciting commodity in the 1990s. Yet he has already suffered groin and pelvic injuries and limps nearly as often as Gordon Greenidge. Premature burn-out is a threat. Wisely, Lancashire have used him sparingly and, wisely, Wasim has paced himself in county games. To avoid killing their golden goose Pakistan must use Wasim no less shrewdly. With Waqar Younis he forms the finest opening attack in Islamic history. But neither Marshall nor Botham was ever worried by strains at so tender an age.

Wasim is a cricketer of his decade, living hard, playing furiously, depending upon his body for survival. May it treat him, and us, kindly.

WAQAR YOUNIS

For Pakistani cricketers as well as politicians, from rags to riches and back is but a small step.

Several years ago, a bedraggled character watched the Pakistan players prepare for a Test match. Nervously he asked for a bowl and impressed the captain who, intolerant of red tape, promptly played him next day.

Tauseef Ahmed, for it was he, swiftly won recognition as a crafty off-spinner. Apparently Abdul Qadir appeared at his first Test wearing gym shoes, his habitual attire at the time, and was denied entry (and no, he wasn't playing at Lord's). Wasim Akram arrived, it seemed, from heaven and he too was rapidly embraced. And now, lo, another diverting cricketer has announced himself and he too is surrounded by exotic legend.

Waqar Younis has the torso and moustache of a man, and yet he has lived but 18 years on this earth. A year ago, he was obscure. Since then he has captured umpteen wickets, most importantly for Surrey and Pakistan.

Raised in Sharjah, where his father was a contract worker, Waqar was unheard of in serious cricket circles until last autumn.

Different tales are told of his sudden emergence. Revealing hitherto unsuspected romanticism, Geoff Arnold, the Surrey coach, says Imran Khan saw Waqar bowling on sand-hills outside Karachi and immediately signed him up. More prosaically, Ian Greig, his county captain, thinks that the Pakistan captain saw him playing while recuperating in front of a television set at home.

Imran, they agree, was struck by Waqar's long, bounding run, by his athleticism, his fitness and his willingness, for here were the raw materials for a fast bowler.

Those gods who grant speed to some and deny it to others had smiled upon Waqar, and he was just the fellow to support Wasim Akram in Australia, notoriously a graveyard for mediocre seamers such as those currently in Pakistan's squad.

Just the fellow, too, to relieve an old warrior of his burden. Imran wanted to concentrate on his captaincy and his batting. Wanted to become an elder statesman in a youthful team, and he could not do that *and* provide the blood and thunder.

Imran took it upon himself to train this colt, for plainly he was not yet ready to race. Working hard in the months before Australia, Waqar developed a smoothly accelerating run and learnt to bend the ball either way and late.

He was learning from a master, for Imran had found ways of swinging even old and curiously battered balls, usually against the shine; ways he had already passed on to Akram; ways now being discovered by hard-pressed English county bowlers, for swing is all the rage.

Waqar quickly impressed Australian batsmen with his hostility, and they thought him as fast as Wasim Akram if not as skilful.

Imran used him in bursts, and often when the ball had lost its gloss. But it was in the Sharjah limited-over tournament that Waqar really caught the eye, taking 17 wickets for 126 runs in 34 overs, convincing everyone of his calibre. Pakistan beat Australia in the final to retain their title, and Waqar was Man of the Series.

It was, of course, only a start. Imran advised his protégé to play some county second eleven cricket this summer so that he might learn to bowl in all conditions, to use cloud and moisture. Sussex turned him away but Surrey, in need of a cutting edge, were more sanguine. Greig saw Waqar bowl in the nets and hurried to register him before others had the chance. He has chosen well, for Waqar has taken a stack of wickets in the first team and shown himself to be a great enthusiast. If allowed, he will bowl all day.

Against Somerset at Weston-super-Mare, Greig used his deadliest weapon sparingly, relying on his spinners, a tactic on which Waqar frowned as if it were soft, as perhaps it was for a man not thinking of tomorrow.

Not that Waqar seemed to be the complaining sort; rather he was quiet and polite. It was just that he wanted to bowl. He was still absorbing a new world into whose more diverting pastimes he is inclined to dip just a toe.

Certainly he was unaware of the consternation his various spells caused both behind the stumps and in front of them. So fast was he, and with so pronounced and bewildering a swing, that Surrey's various wicketkeepers found themselves diving to and fro like goalkeepers in a shoot-out. At times Greig set his fielder so fine at long-leg as to embarrass a sensitive stumper.

But if Waqar provoked such emotions behind the stumps, it was as nothing compared with the alarm he caused in front of them.

Hurtling in from the sight-screen for his bursts of four or five overs, hurling down his outswingers, and every so often a cruel, late inswinger which tended to land on a fellow's toe (Chris Cowdrey has already had one broken), Waqar was decidedly a handful even on the Weston pitch.

Unusually for a fast bowler, he lost no pace when pitching the ball up; perhaps his low trajectory gives him fizz through the air rather than explosion off the pitch.

Comparisons with men such as Marshall, Hadlee and Wasim Akram are, of course, absurd. Waqar is a young, fit, optimistic fast bowler of considerable promise; he is an apprentice who can swing a cricket ball but who is not yet its master. He is an engaging cricketer, an exciting fellow who may, one day, be truly magnificent.

WHITE LIGHTNING

Two years ago, after encountering a spell as sizzling as bacon in a heap of fat, I wrote that Paul Jarvis was the fastest white bowler I had faced, which was, admittedly, like naming Gabriel Garcia Marquez as one's favourite Colombian novelist.

Eyebrows were raised. Had Mike Procter's flailing arms and deadly swing been forgotten? Well, yes actually. And what about Dennis Lillee? Never faced him. Thommo? Never in his pomp. Willis? Only in county cricket. And what about this new bloke Donald, of Bloemfontein and Birmingham? Apparently he has the pace that burns too, like a motorcycle across turf. Never faced him, either.

Now all can be revealed. Allan Donald, fair, lanky, lean and simple without being guileless, is as quick a bowler as any seen in the last 20 years, white or otherwise. Anyone doubting this should have been in my boots at Edgbaston a month ago.

Upon taking guard, respectable batsmen peruse the field – a custom of no earthly use but it is expected, besides which it delays the dreadful moment when a ball has to be faced. Such a perusal did not, on this occasion, detect any sign of life on that Edgbaston field save for Donald and a brace of umpires.

It took a closer scrutiny to find a wicketkeeper and a clutch of slips standing somewhere on the Worcestershire border. To a batsman this was a bad sign. No bowler in the world can have driven his keeper further back. (Not that Mr Piper and colleagues could not be heard!)

Donald is extremely fast. Blessed with a supple body – he can touch his toes with his wrists – he runs smoothly in to unleash deliveries which more resemble a streak of lightning than a roll of thunder, for they are deadly and sudden rather than an elemental force of nature.

By no means is Donald's bowling as brutal as that of Sylvester Clarke or Colin Croft, merchants with unorthodox actions capable of producing explosive deliveries on benign pitches. Donald is cultured and classical, relies on a high arm in the manner of Holding, Snow and Lillee, men who can be fun to face because batsmen can pick up their deliveries easily and judge their pace accordingly. Fun, that is, if only the pitch were four yards longer.

These bowlers have in common an uncluttered and surging run, producing a pace which is pure, unadulterated. They rely upon technique and talent rather than brute force, for their pace is a gift from the gods, not a manufactured product of muscled limbs.

For each of them rhythm is a critical and elusive characteristic; without it they are reduced to mere mortals. With it they can scintillate and destroy. Neither Donald nor these earlier giants are often inclined to indulge in those bouts of ferocity against which the International Cricket Council have taken such a firm stand. They may intimidate by pace and the threat of something nasty, but usually they take wickets with skill.

Besides his suppleness, athleticism is the clue to Donald's pace. Bob Woolmer, the Warwickshire coach, uses a stopwatch to time him as he runs from mark to delivery. At his peak, Donald's run lasts 3.29 sec, but sometimes his legs are heavy and his mind confused so that he trundles in, head back, at a slower 4.11 sec.

Once Woolmer has alerted him to this fact, Donald recaptures his pace and is happy again, for he is a fellow who enjoys bowling fast, a cricketer who dismissed Leicester for 58 in a practice game last April, provoking Peter Willey to ask: 'If he's that quick in a friendly, what's he like when the gloves are off?'

So far as taking wickets goes, Donald relies mostly on slip catches, bruised toes and shattered stumps. He bowls as if bent on blasting his way through such brittle resistance as is offered. Often he bowls a full length, confident that batsmen will have too little time to punish with a drive, even those daring to tread forward. Already he has taken 60 wickets in championship games, and six bags of five wickets to boot, winning games and lifting his side to the top of the table.

Do not suppose, however, that Donald is entirely a creature of gentility. Aroused, he can pepper the middle of a pitch as well as any rival, and did so after one umpire penalised him for catching a ball he had supposed dead in his cap.

He did so again at Edgbaston that time, and managed to hit a variety of parts attached to your correspondent, though seldom the bat. Facing such raw pace, a batsman feels as if he is on a drug, so sharp are his reflexes, self-preservation being a powerful force.

For his county, Donald bowls short spells, for each one is treasured and used to break down a wall which has held for too long, or to widen a breach that has been made. Usually his bursts last four overs, no matter if wickets are falling, and in each Donald rapidly finds his full pace. Being young, he does not stiffen; being used sparingly, he need hold nothing in reserve.

Plainly he is as lethal a bowler as Waqar Younis or Wasim Akram in county cricket. Can he be as effective in the Test arena? Truly great fast bowlers, like Hadlee or Lillee, can act alone, regardless of support. Donald may not quite be ready for this yet, may lack the command of swing and cut to take wickets on slow pitches or when his edge has been blunted by durable Test batsmen.

In county cricket he is protected by his captain and supported by an excellent trio in Small, Munton and Reeve. Time will tell if his South African colleagues are as impressive.

At present Donald is a majestic fast bowler, one who stings like a viper and then withdraws to the foliage. He is magnificent though not yet, I think, great. In many respects he resembles Lillee, yet to stand beside him he too must reveal depths of courage, stamina and resource beyond anything he has yet been called upon to reveal.

LARWOOD'S LEGACY

They called him The Wrecker, The Killer and Murder on Tip Toe. Apparently those awaiting their fate could not hear him as he ran in to bowl. People hooted and screamed at him as he bombarded their heroes, Bill Ponsford, Bill Woodfull and Don Bradman; they wrote vitriolic letters and a judge said the criminal law of assault could be invoked.

So fierce was his attack that relations between countries were imperilled, so uncompromising was his shelling of Australians in 1932–33 that it was too much even for his lords and masters, who, a year later, treated him shabbily, distancing themselves as if he were a renegade.

He never played Test cricket again for he was utterly unprepared to apologise for what he, obeying orders, had done.

At 85 years of age, sprightly, humble, and still speaking in a broad Nottingham accent, Harold Larwood, scourge of Australia, is alive and well and living in Sydney.

Somewhat short-sighted, he potters around at home in his slippers, listening to Harry Secombe and brass band records, polishing his mementos, sipping tea with Lois, his 'Missus' of 63 years, chatting to such children and grandchildren as pop by and otherwise minding his own business, not having left his front gate in years.

If a cricketing chum drops in he will open a few bottles of beer, for Harold shrinks from publicity not from people, and he has always enjoyed an ale, so much so that Douglas Jardine used to instruct Bill Bowes and Maurice Leyland to keep an eye on him of a night, which was easier said than done.

An old man in repose, his battles lost and won, Larwood lives in a small and comfortable house with nothing grand about it, simply a house in a row of like minded houses. He lives without pretension and fuss, in his own way and on his own terms, happy with his lot and determined to live on his merits not on his name.

It is this which makes him the most impressive former cricketer I have met.

Seeing him, no-one could guess he had so tormented Australia all those years ago. A casual visitor, studying his size (5ft 7ins or 1.7m) and deceptively frail body, might mistake him for a retired sweet shop owner. Which he is. Or someone who ran a flower stall, which he did, or a former night watchman or factory worker, all of which he did and all after he was famous.

Only those mementos, of which a silver ashtray presented by Jardine and inscribed 'To Harold for the Ashes 1932 – From a Grateful Skipper' has pride of place, show that this was one of the giants of the game, a man who won a series against overwhelming odds, a man who caused such a rumpus that rules had to be changed, a man so proud that he sacrificed his Test career when they tried to disown him.

Bowes, said of his work in 1932–33: 'To have seen Larwood in Australia is to have witnessed one of the greatest of all sporting occasions.'

Larwood was born in Nuncargate, a mining village in Nottinghamshire. His family was music-minded but Harold was having none of that. He wanted to play cricket and he meant to do so.

From the start, he was a fellow who might be broken but not bent. Accordingly, his father cut out a bat from a hunk of wood and the child began to play morning, noon and night notwithstanding sundry discouraging wallopings from his educators.

He left school as soon as he could and at 13 found work in a local grocery. Scarcely 4ft (1.2m) from tip to toe he lugged bags of flour as big as himself and was once found unconscious under a hundredweight of margarine.

At 14 he was old enough to go down the pit where he worked, stripped to the waist, as a pony driver. Tunnels were only 3ft 8ins (1.1m) and as he slogged away, his body and back gathered a wiry strength.

In his spare time he caddied at the local golf club, augmenting the family income, and played cricket, bowling in sandshoes, for his local club.

At 17, Joe Hardstaff Snr, a county cricketer who lived nearby, took him for a county trial for which his father forked out £9 in 'new clobber'.

Larwood's pace surprised the professionals and he was offered terms at 32 shillings a week, precisely the wage he was paid down the mines. His father berated him for not asking for more but Harold was mild by temperament.

When picked for England in 1926 he said to Arthur Carr, his captain: 'Surely, Mr Carr, I'm not good enough.' To this day he speaks of the old amateurs as Mr Warner and Mr Jardine, out of politeness not servility.

By 1925 he was a regular county cricketer. Arthur Carr, captain of Nottingham and England, could see his potential. Fearful of a breakdown, he used Larwood in short bursts and twice a week he took Harold and his partner (and great chum) Bill Voce out for a steak and as much beer as they could sink.

Carr said of his fast pair: 'You can lead 'em anywhere but you cannot drive them an inch.'

So it was throughout with Larwood. In 1926 Larwood made his England debut and in his second Test helped the recalled Wilfred Rhodes, 48, to win the deciding Ashes Test at The Oval. Larwood took 6–116 and Rhodes 6–79.

A year later he married in secret, and that summer finished on top of the national bowling averages as he was to do in five of the next ten seasons.

In 1928–29 he toured Australia with England and, hampered by a thigh injury and a wonky knee, took 14 wickets none too cheaply, never once trapping the new fellow who smiled mercilessly as he walked out to bat, Bradman.

Bradman went to England in 1930 and gave a dreadful hammering to all bowlers. Only one chink was found in his armour. Bowling on a wet pitch Gubby Allen had forced Bradman to back away and taken his wicket cheaply. Upon hearing of this, Larwood said: 'If that little bugger can do that to him, what might I do?'

He yearned for the day when he might bowl to Bradman on hard, fast tracks where bat and ball had an equal chance.

He yearned for the day when he was fully fit, for he had been carrying injuries during the 1930 series in which he took four expensive wickets.

Plainly a strategy had to be found to stop Bradman, because Tests were played to a finish in those days and he could destroy England.

Jardine, appointed captain of the 1932–33 tour, decided to sharpen an old tactic by bowling at leg stump and pitching short with five men around the bat. It was a tactic which demanded precision, pace and hostility, a tactic which relied almost entirely on Larwood for only Voce could offer appropriate support.

Bodyline was used a fraction of the time, only when it mattered, and it worked. Larwood took 33 wickets at 19 apiece and England won 4–1. A film of Larwood in full flight reveals a lithe skipping run of 14 paces, a rhythmic gathering of arms and legs into a final leap, an elastic and electrifying whirl at delivery followed by a scraping of the ground with a long right arm, a scraping which left knuckles bleeding, and a follow-through which took him to within yards of his enemies. First impressions of a jerky action are mere tricks of the camera for longer inspection shows a fluency seldom rivalled.

On the hard grounds of Australia Larwood found he could skim the ball like a pebble on water and with as unpredictable a bounce.

Bumpers leapt too high so he pitched short of a length and made the ball rear wickedly at ribs. Bodies were battered and men hit, Woodfull and Bert Oldfield badly, though neither when leg theory was being bowled.

Early in his spell he used to grip the ball lightly and bowl outswingers to an orthodox field, but shine did not last long in those days – because of hand stitching, Larwood says – and soon he concentrated on break-backs delivered from wide of the crease at leg stump.

Bradman began backing away, using the open spaces to counterattack he said, a tactic which caused dismay in Australian ranks and a psychological triumph for England who could argue, rightly or wrongly, that Bradman was scared.

Certainly the boy from Bowral was reduced to mere mortality by this barrage. Jack Fingleton thought Larwood 'anxious to claim a hit on Bradman' in the final Test, which he duly did, Bradman having survived intact that far.

Larwood did not want to play in this last Test but Jardine meant to rub home his advantage. Larwood broke down in the second innings and was not allowed to leave the field while 'the little bastard's in'.

When Bradman was out, the pair walked off together, silently. In the dressing-room Larwood squeezed blood from his socks and his foot was black from toe to heel. He never played Test cricket again.

His foot did not heal properly, preventing him from playing in

1933, and he was never quite the same again, though easily good enough to represent England.

Then MCC said he would not be considered for the 1934 Ashes series unless he apologised, which Larwood refused to do. He had been horribly, if predictably, let down by the establishment in a very English way. Disgusted, he declared himself unfit; Voce did not play either and Australia swept all before them.

Larwood retired in 1938 with 1,427 first-class wickets to his credit, and just 78 Test victims. His reputation as the greatest depends largely upon that controversial series when he was fit and finally given a chance. He should have been born 20 years later.

After the War, Larwood opened a sweet shop in Blackpool to which Fingleton paid a visit in 1950. Harold was barely scraping a living for his family, rationing was still in force and he said he was contemplating emigration. Fingleton made the arrangements, built a house in Randwick and organised temporary accommodation in a hotel until it was ready.

Larwood, his wife and five daughters arrived to a warm welcome and found themselves paying a mere £16 a week for their digs.

Only later did they realise that Ben Chifley, ALP leader and recently Prime Minister, had paid half their bill out of his own pocket. Had he known Larwood would never have accepted such generosity.

He was offered all sorts of jobs in business but said: 'I'd rather shovel muck than do a charity job.'

Whereupon he found work as a nightwatchman, a storekeeper and later in a fruit drinks factory beside lots of 'new Australians'.

Happy in the sunshine, happy to be rid of England's class system, Larwood settled into his new home and never regretted his move.

Defining himself, Larwood simply says: 'I always wanted to be the best at whatever I did.' He was.

GREAT SIR GARFIELD

I FIRST saw Gary Sobers in the flesh at Taunton in 1971. Of course, I had watched him countless times on television, in the 1963, 1966 and 1969 Test series for example, but somehow never live before. Somerset – some things remain ever the same – were chasing the John Player League title. A massive, throbbing crowd had come to watch this crucial game. Just the thing to stimulate the aged, slightly lame champion.

His appearance was sleek as a greyhound, slim, graceful in movement, yet almost hobbling in that strange, hiccuppy walk of his.

Sobers took a blinding catch, four wickets, scored 73 not out and guided his Nottinghamshire team to victory. A performance by a virtuoso, an all-rounder who, when roused, could dominate a game to an extent matched only by Mike Procter in top flight cricket.

To my young eyes the most impressive aspect of this performance was its discipline. It was not a spectacular, chancy effort. Sobers simply bowled straight, and batted with intelligence and care. With wise humility, he treated Somerset's best bowlers, Tom Cartwright and Brian Langford, with respect. Cartwright even slipped a few balls past his bat. But as these men finished their spells Sobers was still in, biding his time. He tore into the change bowling with relish, ending the game with a magnificent straight six off Bajan fast-bowler Hallam Moseley. This stroke, executed from the back foot, is in the repertoire of very few men. Viv Richards played it at Hove against John Snow, but then he can bat a bit, too. Anyhow, not bad for a man suffering from arthritic knees. What on earth could he do earlier in his career?

Somerset's hopes were destroyed once again, yet no-one could resent it. Even the most trenchant cider-saturated supporters enjoyed the quality of Sobers' cricket. And it was all done with such grace and charm. For goodness' sake, he was smiling and joking most of the time. It is hard to despise any enemy who is so pleasant; it quite disturbs one's prejudices – rather as if the Red Indians collected rags for refugees, the Sheriff of Nottingham took in orphans, or the Germans ate liquorice all-sorts instead of children.

Sobers continued to play for several seasons after that genial disruption of Somerset's ambitions. He never seemed fully fit again; the well-oiled engine never purred quite so smoothly. He remained the best cricketer in the world almost until he retired, but lost that little sparkle which suggested he might, in his prime, have been the most brilliant cricketer in the history of the game.

As late as 1973 Sobers returned to the fray, leaner and more arthritic still. He managed to hobble to the crease with sufficient life to take several vital wickets, equal the Test match catching record (six in the match at Lord's), and score a controlled 150 in the final Test. Not bad for an old man who, were he a horse, would have been put to grass or put down long before.

Incidentally, in the Third Test came one of cricket's more dispiriting moments. The sight of G. St A. Sobers resuming an innings interrupted by injury on 109 with his team's score 568 for five. Time to throw in the towel, the selectors, the wife, the car and the kids. Time to retire to some Siberian camp where a bowler's lot is a bit less arduous.

Sir Garfield St Aubyn Sobers of Barbados, South Australia, Nottinghamshire, West Indies and Rest of the World. Beyond doubt a cricketing genius.

Genius emerges in many shapes and forms. Keith Miller was a maverick, unpredictable. Ian Botham is aggressive, instinctive, irrational. Don Bradman was ruthless, masterful. Sobers stands in memory as having been, like a classical composer (Mozart, say), beautifully correct. His bowling captured rhythm and relaxation, not a jink to disturb the rippling effect. This in stark contrast to the Rolling Stones ferocity of Charlie Griffith, or the fearsome, awe-inspiring approach of Wesley Hall.

Sobers was a genius of inspired orthodoxy; he was a cricketer's cricketer. People enjoyed playing against him, as one might have enjoyed playing tennis against Rod Laver, or fighting Muhammad Ali (ignoring the painful result of this particular foray). Sobers combined flawless technique and gentle manners. He was the master in that talented, explosive West Indies team of the mid 1960s.

Rohan Kanhai could be inspired, Seymour Nurse elegant,

Conrad Hunte sometimes solid, sometimes brilliant, Basil Butcher superb off the back foot, Clive Lloyd could plunder, Hall and Griffith explode. Sobers, like Frank Worrell whom he so much admired, appeared graceful, lithe and reliable. Less spectacular than some, less of a wizard than others, Sobers was the bastion of the team. Whatever company he kept, Sobers was the man you had to dismiss. Possibly that is one reason he batted at six for the West Indies. There was always Sobers to come, a reassuring thought for some of the more volatile men higher in the order. And a depressing one for the bowlers. Dispose of Hunte, Kanhai, Butcher, Nurse and Lloyd, and in comes Sir Gary.

Gary Sobers batted as he bowled, with fluency and very straight. He seemed to lean on the ball with arms and wrists extending, to flash the ball to the boundary without apparent effort. Most memorably that graceful cut behind point, and the off-drive on the up which sizzled through covers already standing 10 yards deeper than usual. I gather from C. L. R. James's writing that these strokes were referred to in Barbados as 'not a man move' shots. With Sobers the ball either went straight to the fielder or 'not a man move'. There really would have been no point.

I well recall Sobers' fluent grace. Not that he did not often simply stand up and belt the ball with fierce power, for, as Learie Constantine advised Bradman: 'Sobers hits the ball as consistently hard as anyone I've ever seen.' It is just that one remembers his lazy elegance rather than his vicious hitting.

Sobers rarely displayed the mean destructive power of Clive Lloyd or Viv Richards at their best. When this formidable pair are 'in' a demon possesses them, like a heavyweight champion destroying an opponent like Joe Frazier, 'steamed up', demolishing a challenger.

Sir Gary scored just as quickly, hit the ball every bit as hard as Lloyd or Richards, yet never appeared to be 'steamed up'. His batting resembled golf rather than prize fighting. He strolled to the crease; he never hurried between the wickets; he rarely darted out to spinners; he often smiled, chatting to Alan Knott even in Test matches.

Just once in a while, though, Sobers was overtaken by an angry demoralising mood. His most famous innings was also his most furious. That astonishing 254 for a World XI against Australia at Melbourne in 1972 stands, with Stan McCabe's 232 at Nottingham in 1938, as an example of inspired, destructive batting. Something must have possessed Sobers that day, some set-back in his personal life. He batted with the fury of an avenging angel – hell hath no fury, we soon understood, with Sobers roused.

Bowlers may be thankful that Sobers' genius at the crease usually found expression in mere domination of the attack; the days when he took batting into apparently impossible realms were, inevitably, rare. His most memorable assault, apart from that 254, was the 132 he made against Benaud's Australia in the famous tied match at Brisbane 1961. Riled by suggestions that he could not play Benaud's leg-spin, Sobers tore into a talented Australian attack, scoring his century in even time in a convincing assertion of his mastery.

Sir Gary's bowling, too, stands in memory for its languid rhythm, its late effortless movement. For several years Sobers was the most lethal new ball bowler in the world. His wicked in-dip trapped many batsmen in front of their stumps before their eyes were in. The run-up was panther-like in its grace, with the right arm pointing high towards the skies, and the pivot of the shoulders which brought surprising pace and encouraged swing.

Contests between Gary Sobers and Geoffrey Boycott were especially lively as Sobers sought after a break in that stern defence. Boycott, straight bat resisting the 'snake', a battle of wits between skilled opponents without a hint of intimidation or malpractice. Each appreciated the other's ability, each knew the other's purpose, Sobers to trap Boycott in front, or to persuade him to play at a wider delivery and edge to the slips, Boycott to ignore the out-swinger, keep at bay the 'nip-backer' and drive the half-volley through the sparsely populated outfield.

Gary Sobers was an ever-attacking bowler. He bowled at the stumps with a ring of supporting slips. He was prepared to concede runs for the chance of a wicket. He rarely bowled in defensive vein. His spirit did not run that way. Probably this is one reason he was more comfortable in his faster style, rather than in his essentially defensive orthodox spin.

And he never bowled a bouncer ('What, never?' 'Well, hardly ever!'). His wickets were taken through skill, defeating the batsman by movement or sudden change of pace. Few of Sobers's victims were caught at long-leg off a bouncer, few opponents were forced to duck and weave for their very lives.

As a result of this open-hearted approach, Gary Sobers's 235

Test wickets cost 34 runs each. This contrasts with Trueman's 307 wickets at 21, Bedi's 266 at 28, Gibbs's 309 wickets at 29 and Hall's 192 wickets at 26. Sobers could be expensive, but he could also be devastating. Left-arm pace bowlers seem able to produce occasional bursts during which they are utterly unplayable. Alan Davidson, Gary Gilmour, and even, in county cricket, Malcolm Nash, have days when their swing is so late, so controlled that opponents fall before them like wheat before the harvester.

Most often Sobers produced these electrifying spells in England, where his swing found most encouragement and where the full length to which he naturally bowled was most appropriate. Headingley, in particular, suited Sobers for, in 1966 and 1969, he reduced England to disarray with spells of five for 41 and five for 42.

Not bad for someone who entered international cricket as a left-arm spin bowler.

The pace bowling did not begin until 1960, and only emerged as a major force in Test cricket in England in 1963. Sobers continued to bowl his spinners as well, of course, often partnering Lance Gibbs in helpful conditions. His orthodox spin was accurate, with well-concealed variations, but Sobers always appeared happiest and most dangerous as a swing bowler.

As if this were insufficient contribution Sobers developed, for a few startling years, an inkling to bowl left-arm googlies and chinamen (if these deliveries are different!). He bowled these rather as Victor Borge plays the piano, with a smile, with talent, with varying degrees of success and with a twinkle in the eye suggesting that he could bowl properly, really.

And, if all that were not enough, it is easily forgotten that Sobers was a fielder of the utmost brilliance. Many folk remember instinctive run-outs by Sobers at short-leg to Lance Gibbs. A leg glance, a rapid stop and flick back to the stumps leaving the batsman stranded as he set off for a single. As an unobtrusive short-leg to Gibbs, or second slip to Hall and Griffith, Sobers moved with lightning decisiveness. He held 110 catches in Test cricket. Goodness alone knows how many he would have caught had he not been bowling most of the time.

If this creates the impression of a staggeringly, unfairly talented man, then it is no more than the truth. But Sobers was more than that. He was, in essence, a *good* cricketer. He was not wild or lucky, though certainly he was dropped in the slips more than most, no doubt because he edged the ball harder than most. Sobers was not prone, as Ian Botham sometimes is, to take heroic, outrageous liberties. He was a determined, intelligent cricketer.

He bowled accurately and to a full length because that is good cricket. He refused to bowl bouncers, or to bowl away from the wickets, because that is bad cricket. He did not advance down the pitch to spinners because he did not need to; the risk was unnecessary. He flashed at the ball outside the off-stump with joyous abandon, yet even this stroke was calculated, as much as Ian Chappell reckoned that his hook brought him sufficient runs to justify the occasional dismissal.

Sobers was an excellent cricketer; a superb craftsman on bad wickets; as adept against fast bowling as he was against spin. He scored over 8,000 runs in Test cricket at an average of nearly 58, despite going in at six as the team's all-rounder and captain. Usually Sobers chased runs almost as soon as he came in, and once in a while he fell early, flashing at a wide half-volley. The physical demands of bowling so many overs forced Sir Gary to adopt an aggressive approach to batting. His team could not afford him to exhaust himself with unnecessarily long innings. And often, like Procter and Botham, Sobers would stroll to the crease still weary from the labours of bowling. It is remarkable that Sobers scored so many runs consistently for so long. No other heavy scorer in Test cricket endured such harsh demands far beyond the world of batting.

Gary Sobers could, of course, play long, carefully-constructed innings. Circumstances sometimes required prolonged resistance. And no cricketer can truly be designated 'great' unless he can save games as well as win them. Sobers's most famous rescuing mission was his partnership with his young, inexperienced cousin David Holford at Lord's in 1966. They came together with half the team gone, and a slender lead of nine runs on the board. Conditions were helping England's battery of seamers, Higgs, Knight, Jeff Jones and Basil d'Oliveira. Sobers launched a counter attack, driving vividly and forcing England captain Colin Cowdrey onto the defensive. With the initiative regained, Sobers and Holford collected runs carefully until, safety achieved, they cut loose again, enabling Sobers to declare at 369 for five. Sobers 163, Holford 105.

Sobers regards this as his most valuable innings. Certainly it was one of his most disciplined. England never scented victory again until, with the series in the bag, Close led his team to a massive victory as first Graveney and Murray, and then Snow and Higgs, forged vital partnerships. Ever-generous Sobers refused to attribute this heavy defeat to relaxation, preferring the view that his team had been beaten fair and square.

With this skill, and the excellence of technique and temperament, one wonders just how many runs Sobers would have scored, how many wickets he would have taken, had he been able to give his full energies to one discipline or the other.

THE ART OF CRICKET

IT was odd to be asked by the *Sydney Morning Herald* to write about the art of cricket on a day when black men dressed in red clothes and white men dressed in blue clothes were doing battle for a silver cup on a green pitch with floodlights blazing and sight screens blackened so that the white ball could be seen by batsmen wearing cages on their heads. A subdued sport of green and white has erupted into a wildness of brilliant colour. A game of sheltered upbringing has exploded into the bright lights and sinuous temptations of the modern world.

The art of cricket? What could this mean? Had the paper taken leave of its senses? Then, dimly, through the mists of time, remembrance returned, a remembrance of Sobers and Graveney, of Greg Chappell and Graeme Pollock, mesmeric cricketers one and all. And a remembrance, too, of words catching the grace of Hobbs and Kippax, and the kindness of Oldfield and Ranjitsinhji.

Yes, cricket is artistic, the most artistic of all games. Oh, it is played by dullards at times, and occasionally, reading about it, you'd think it was as artistic as a nest of cockroaches eating their supper, but Cardus, Ray Robinson, Arlott, Pinter, Betjeman, and so many other men of sensitivity have understood it, sympathised with its victims and written about it. So many men have found a peculiar satisfaction in the game.

However it might seem sitting glumly in a press box surrounded by the clacking of word processors and contemplating the compulsory excitement of a one-day game, cricket is a loved and beautiful game. Has this art survived the move into the marketplace? Can a game in the hands of hard-headed financiers nevertheless be called artistic? It can.

The essence of the game has not changed. A rose is a rose for all that. Cricket is a difficult, frustrating and frequently witless game, but though the rules have been changed it has not lost its smattering of breathtaking moments nor its occasional geniuses who, scarcely realising it, follow a tradition and give immense pleasure to their audience not so much by their achievements as by their methods.

No other sport rivals cricket's instinctive art. Others are more spinetingling, rugged, fascinating, disciplined, fast and tense. In comparison, cricket is a route march which occasionally passes through leafy lanes and majestic forests. As a competition between teams it is frequently disappointing, can be spoilt by rain, and ruined by the players. It can last five days and still end without resolution, for it is a ridiculous game, absurdly long and ludicrously indecisive.

It survives because of the enduring appeal of its vignettes, because of the singular way in which character and beauty find expression within its confines. No moderately sane person could consider it satisfactory as a whole. It is a deceitful, hypnotic, treacherous game which has appalling faults and extraordinary qualities.

All-in wrestling might be more fun, but it is not poetic. Rugby is an invigorating game, but it does not inspire paintings. Musicians are not moved to compose as a golfer strikes a ball onto the green.

Bodies thudding to the floor to be trapped in arm locks, a prop forward driving to the line, and a chip creeping to the flag – these are tense, telling moments which are cheered by spectators caught in the drama of the competition. They are skilful and courageous reactions to tension, and the players deserve the applause for their temporary triumphs. But wrestling, rugby and golf crowds do not blink at the beauty of their sports; they do not contemplate them in this way. They are not games of wonder; rather they are contests between rivals.

Cricket is the most beautiful of games, which is why it is celebrated in verse, on canvas and in music. On the field, some of the players are able to move as if in a ballet without losing their effectiveness. Players dressed in white (well, usually anyhow) move into neat gymnastic positions against a back-cloth of grass and a kaleidoscope of colour and a cacophony of noise blaring behind the fence. It is a bizarre medieval scene, a mixture of ritual, entertainment, sport and art. And it has not lost its appeal, will never do so, for it is intrinsic and beyond the everchanging laws.

Nothing is more graceful in this or any other game than an off drive played by David Gower. A rhythmic drift towards the ball is followed by a smooth sweep through a straight line which sends the ball scorching across the turf. A Gower drive is a mixture of delicate, unobtrusive footwork and a fluent swing which ends in a comforting thump as wood and leather meet.

This game is satisfying because it is a game of straight lines. Cricket demands them of its players and those who defy it risk failure. Ugly angles and jagged lines are rejected by the classical technique required in those without genius. As if by accident, cricket pleases the eye as well as the mathematical and aesthetic mind.

Nor are the graceful and classical movements on the field the only ingredients in cricket's appeal. Is anything in sport more tantalising than a duel between a spinner and a batsman prepared to use his feet? When Edmonds bowls to Dean Jones, there occurs an enthralling battle of wits, one man stepping forward boldly, ready to strike, and determined to dictate to his rival, who, full of cunning, is using flight and guile in an effort to sneak one past the bat.

These exchanges are secret, private to the cognoscenti who alone can understand the peculiar duel. Cricketers and spectators are in constant conversation as the movement of the players reveals to the audience their plans, worries, hopes and fears. The uninformed will not grasp the significance of these strange events, will not understand what Edmonds is endeavouring to do nor why Jones is dancing with such vigour as the cat and mouse do battle.

And, because the game stops and starts so often, because a day's play consists of 540 separate and yet dependent incidents, students can swap opinions, comment upon the action to their friends, and predict the course of events to follow.

Cricket is a game that asks much of its followers; it expects them to join in. A good crowd recognises mastery and beauty and applauds them irrespective of whether a run has been scored, a wicket taken or the game advanced in any way. Cricket catches the eye and satisfies the wit. And at best it is full of pleasing movements and ideas.

But this is not a nice game. It is a temptress, a Cleopatra of a game. Herein lies its greatest appeal. Its art is elusive. Cricket cannot be mastered. Like a seductress it moves away, cocking a finger, asking you to follow and yet warning you as to the consequences. On the field tragedy follows hard upon triumph, ease and discomfort sit side by side.

Cricket is dangerous and not to be trusted. One minute it is enticing, rhythmic and charming, and the next it betrays you. This is a fragile game which treats its players unkindly. So many cricketers are insecure, lured by taste occasionally experienced and then let down by it. This game gives its players hope in a moment and then chastises them, throwing them back onto the heap. For a moment it is in our grasp and then it has escaped. Hardly anyone who has played the game has not, even if only once, done something artistic, something upon which Trumper and Bedi could scarcely improve. A late cut dashes to the boundary and at once the batsman realises he has got it right, his body fulfilling the idea in his mind. This illusion, these sweet moments, are part of the game's trap; the dreadfulness usually follows.

This is why the poets and the writers came to the game. They recognised its wickedness and its bloodymindedness as well as its beauty. So many cricketers, their careers behind them, have committed suicide. Bored by ordinariness, unable to find a new refuge or simply despairing of the future, they choose their moment and put an end to it all.

A long list could be drawn of cricketers who have taken their lives. It is not a coincidence but a terrible revelation about cricket and cricketers. The game does not break them, rather they are drawn by temperament to it, finding in it an expression of their precarious characters. They play the game, try to master it and occasionally succeed, joining a fraternity of men no less frustrated and no less in search of a reliable method. They try to find an answer where there is none. Try to find a stone where there is only sand.

Cricket is a game played on the edges of nerves. It requires men of stoical and stout temperament, yet attracts players with artistic yearnings who hover around it as a moth hovers around a flame. Spectators sense this vulnerability. A man who scored 100 yesterday falls for a duck, and a cricketer invincible one year fails the next. They sense that cricket is a prickly game which hurls misfortune and joy at its players without warning and expects them to bear each with fortitude. Spectators understand too that some men of artistic temperament are peculiarly tempted toward the game and yet are uniquely unsuited to its changes.

These are the arts and the attractions of cricket, some of them obvious to a casual follower, some of them hidden and apparent only to those who have tried themselves. Tomorrow's match at the SCG is not merely a competition between two international teams. It is an occasion on which men will be stretched and tested, it is a game of sudden movements, and a game of a beauty that endures despite the odd things done to it.

REMARKABLE
RUN-MAKERS

BOYCOTT

A couple of years ago Geoffrey Boycott and I found ourselves captaining opposing county teams in Middlesbrough. Boycott won the toss and as we returned to the pavilion he said, 'There's 5,000 people here. They've come to see me bat, so we'll bat first.'

Boycott fitted into Yorkshire cricket, though not into Yorkshire's cricket team. Toward the end of his career he'd appear on the field at a quarter to ten to begin his preparations for the day. 'Oh Christ,' you'd think, 'there's that bugger Boycott.' Sometimes you suspected that Yorkshire lads took a similar view.

He'd follow a routine of exercises while the rest of the lads had a knock-up. His colleagues were beer-and-skittles men, a few pints of an evening, a vindaloo to round it off. Boycott sipped Perrier water and ate washed vegetables.

His meals, his clothes, his hair and his briefcase were etched and precise. At the crease his body was poised as if its shapes had been sculptured, with straight lines, tight angles and a left elbow pointing religiously to the sky. His movements were sharp and defined, like a character in a cartoon.

If he was playing for Bradford Boilermakers he'd still graft for his runs, never, never letting his game slip. His concept of batting had a purity about it. Everything in his life was dedicated to tightening his technique. Batting, batting . . . to him the word had a solemnity about it. Later he built a wall of barbed wire around his house. From the start his batting was barbed.

Behind his forward defence he built his statistics, collecting his centuries, hardly ever losing his way. Once at Cambridge he scored 207 not out. For six hours he did not hit a ball in the air, did not hit a ball into the ground so that it bounced away. Every stroke streaked across the turf and between fieldsmen. He did not appear to be concentrating. His mind was utterly absorbed, so he did not need to focus it on the bowling.

He did buckle occasionally, and could panic if flaws were exposed in his game. Left-arm seamers troubled him because he was so side-on and could not easily read their swing or their angle. Sobers, Solkar and Somerset's Mark Davis dismissed him cheaply quite a few times. Usually, though, his game appeared impregnable.

Spinners, in particular, rarely defeated him as he read their line and length, understood their variations of flight with uncanny accuracy. Once Vic Marks did fool him, causing Boycott to be stumped. Next morning he stared at the pitch for ten minutes trying to work out where the ball had bounced. Eventually he found the spot by which time Vic had joined him. 'Ah lad,' he said, 'that's where it pitched and then it turned too much.' It was as if a great puzzle had been solved.

From Sutcliffe to Hutton to Boycott the tradition of Yorkshire batting endures. Each man was a master of technique. Boycott may be the last of the English masters, for these are impatient times full of bonus points and Sunday slashes. But, though the game has changed, cricketers have not. Professionals who do not particularly like Boycott respect his batting immensely for its clarity and its judgement. Maybe the tradition is not so much in conflict with the combativeness of Close and Bairstow. Maybe it is simply in conflict with the times.

GAVASKAR

India's captain, Sunil Gavaskar, is a batsman of genius, a man of impish brilliance who has steeled his technique so that it is as impeccable as a diamond.

He has scored more than 8,000 runs in Test cricket despite carrying the burden of his nation's hopes from the time he first annihilated the West Indian bowling in 1971 with scores of 65, 67, 116, 64 not out, 117 not out, 124 and 220.

A friend once said he hoped he had not added to the weight on Gavaskar by requesting a century. Gavaskar replied that as he had 800 million people already expecting a hundred he did not suppose one more would make any difference.

Despite this pressure he has scored 30 Test centuries, breaking Bradman's record against the West Indies in 1983.

Moreover, although he is widely regarded as a careful batsman he has played several one-day innings of incredible virtuosity.

In 1980 Gavaskar tamed Daniel, Van der Bijl, Selvey, Edmonds and Emburey of Middlesex to reach 128 in 38 overs.

In this innings he lifted the first ball from Van der Bijl (a 6ft 7in fast bowler) over the bowler's head and it bounced a metre inside the boundary.

Although a fragility has crept into his game, Gavaskar's best efforts can be matched only by the West Indies' Viv Richards.

In the 1980s Gavaskar has not collected runs with his former efficiency. He used to bat as unsympathetically as a tax man on a Monday.

In his pomp there was a sturdy air about him at the crease – as though he had booked for bed and breakfast. He would hoard runs, darting twos and threes when one was not looking.

He would be on 23, and after 30 minutes in which nothing much seemed to happen he would be 47. He had the gift of concentrating without apparent effort, a gift of absorption he shared with very few – Geoff Boycott and Len Hutton among them.

Gavaskar never studies the scoreboard and never asks the time.

These are irrelevancies. He wants to deal with the next ball and the one after.

He is not as single-minded these days. Maybe years of continuous Test cricket have drained his reserves or perhaps age has slowed his reflexes.

He appears to reach for the ball more often. These days he fidgets and flicks and can appear quite an ordinary batsman.

Nevertheless, he contributed two staggering innings in recent years.

In 1981 he led India's chase of 435 at The Oval. Only two Test teams have reached 400 to win a match – Bradman's in 1948 and Gavaskar's in 1971, and England had declared confident of a quick victory.

Gavaskar batted for nine hours without error, collecting 220 runs, and lost his wicket in the last frantic unavailing dash.

Last season in India he had an epic duel with Malcolm Marshall. The West Indians had arrived in India determined to avenge their World Cup defeat, which they did by winning 5-0 in the one-day series and 3-0 in the Tests.

Marshall bowled at terrifying pace over upon over. His venom was directed with particular vigour at Gavaskar, still a prized victim.

Several times Gavaskar fell to him early – once first ball. He hit a dashing 90 on a bad pitch, and a careful 100, but approaching the final Test Marshall was ahead on points and Indian spirits were low.

At last Gavaskar, angry at the bombardment, reached his best. In the final game, batting in a sun hat, he marched out and smashed Marshall's first three deliveries to the boundary.

At once the crowd began calling: 'Never awaken the sleeping tiger.'

Marshall switched to around the wicket, the better to pound Gavaskar's body. Gavaskar took the bumpers on the chest and, without flinching, staring at Marshall.

For 1½ hours Marshall tore in to be met by a merciless counter-attack. Eventually the bowler retired to the boundary exhausted, whereupon Gavaskar quietly continued his innings awaiting his adversary's return.

Even on 236 Gavaskar moved in behind Marshall, treating him with disdain as if to ask who the master was now. By all accounts it was his masterpiece. It must have been – his mother has it on video.

BORDER

ALLAN Border is a genius. For years, here and elsewhere, he has been portrayed as a Mosman battler, as a bonzer bloke who made good, as a doughty warrior who has defied a want of talent to conquer his world. Because he lacks panache and charisma he has been judged an old sweat, one who never really had the soupcon of inspiration demanded by genius.

Border has played his part in this fallacy because it fits his assessment of himself as a plain, ordinary fellow, a man entirely without poetry, a thrifty cricketer who could hack out a few runs, bowl a few innocent lobs and field such balls as entered his patch.

And it has all been utter nonsense. To repeat, Border is as much a genius as ever were Viv Richards, David Gower or Ian Botham; his genius takes a different form, that is all. Rather like the Duke of Wellington, his superiority over other men consists 'rather in the perfection of those qualities which he pre-eminently possesses than in their variety or extent'. His genius lies in judgment, in attention to detail, in his consistency and in his ability to handle any sort of bowling on any sort of pitch. Oh, he has no flash, cannot delight with a sudden air plucked from the clouds but since when have frivolity and genius been bedfellows?

In some men talent is captured in a moment, a Gower off-drive, a Richards flick off his toes; with Border it is rather the entire building which provokes our wonder than the dainty or extraordinary which adorn it. Christopher Wren was not considered less of an architect because St Paul's is robust.

Border has been underestimated because we identify genius with volatility, even brittleness, see it in a Paul Gascoigne goal or a daring pot by Alex 'Hurricane' Higgins, fail to see it in the relentlessness of Steve Davis or the regularity of Colin Meads, for these are plain fellows who never make us gasp. Dammit, they are not fragile enough to be geniuses.

Evidently Allan Border also holds his powers in no high regard. Take his bowling. It is, in truth, if not a load of tripe at least a barrowful of turnips and would not trouble a blacksmith in a bush game. And what does this blessed fellow do? He bowls out the West Indians to win a Test match, a feat beyond any contemporary save a couple. He even rolls over an apologetic arm in limited-over games and, 20, wickets fall to him. Is this not the same magic which has for years been detected in the golden arm attached to Ian Botham, noted cricketer and pantomime artiste?

Take his fielding. Border does not think much of it, moves himself from the slips whenever he can, giving precedence to Mark Taylor, Terry Alderman, and even Greg Matthews. And yet he has taken more catches for Australia than any cricketer and dropped precious few. Moreover his last three throws at the stumps have all hit their target as if guided by radar. He ran out Wayne Larkins in Sydney and nearly dismissed Graham Gooch and Gower, too, all with throws made on the run and with one stump in sight. Simply, Border has a knack shared by Botham and Richards of seizing a moment, a knack which in him we do not notice for he does not hold the gazing eye.

Take his batting. Since time immemorial batsmen, and people, have appeared in two sorts – nomadic and settler. Nomads pillage, raise merry hell wherever they go, slaughter their enemies, pinch their crops, then move restlessly away to terrorise other victims. Viv Richards, Dean Jones and David Gower are, in their various ways, nomads, living on their wits, scorning those who put down roots, living on the edge. Allan Robert Border is a settler, one who tends his cattle, encloses his property, grumpily pays his dues, minds his business and ekes out a harsh living, never giving up, enduring the seasons as they turn.

It is this lack of drama, this want of vision, which has misled us. Border never asks us to join him on a journey, never engages our emotions, asks no favour of us. He wins respect for his pragmatism, admiration for his skills but he never provokes wonder, does not try to, does not think of himself in that league.

But CONSIDER his record. In 118 tests he has scored nearly 9,000 runs at an average around 54. He has also turned in just as many extraordinary performances as more illustrious contemporaries. Defying overwhelming odds and a ferocious assault upon his body he scored 98 and 100 in the Trinidad Test of 1983–4, single-handedly turning the Ashes of defeat into the glory of rescue, saving again with Alderman by his side. Everyone recognises this as one of cricket's greatest efforts, this in a game which never forgets its moments of inspiration.

A season earlier in Melbourne he was joined by Jeff Thomson, the mother and father of tailenders, with Australia still needing 83 runs to beat England. In one of cricket's most electrifying finishes Border nagged and punched away until his team was three runs short of a famous victory, whereupon Thomson edged Botham to slip as all Australia sighed in disappointment. Was not this the work of a man possessed by genius? Was ever calculation so superbly executed?

He has scored hundreds in Pakistan and India as well, for Border travels well, does his duty in every clime, will do so as long as his legs will carry him for he is not one to rest upon his achievements, rather 'he marches along to the end, heading such youthful guardians as have sprung to life around him' (the Duke of Wellington again). Lesser men may complain of pitches and Delhi belly. Border seldom seeks the sanctuary of excuses, concentrates instead upon working to win, for above all he likes winning. He never tires of it, for like batting it is a drug, one which lured him away from the beach of his boyhood.

Paul Pritchard, a colleague at Essex, certainly regards Border as a genius and recalls him playing an extraordinary innings against Tony Merrick, a West Indian quickie, on a nasty pitch in Birmingham. Border has been sconed in the first innings and his head was reeling as he took guard a day later, despite which he constructed a magnificent hundred. Another time, studying an especially green county pitch, he announced he could not imagine himself even breaking his duck. To no-one's surprise save his own, he scored 150. It is a part of Border's secret that he is better than he thinks he is, and accordingly, lives within his allowance scarcely realising he is doing so. Perhaps this characteristic has stopped him daring to play more match-winning innings, for commonly he attributes to others qualities he holds in higher degree.

He is, of course, aware of limitations and was for years apt to drop himself down the order in one-day cricket because he could not carve a ball pitching beyond off stump over mid-wicket and accordingly considered himself too stuffy. Now, persuaded by friends, he realises he has enormous strengths, too, strengths tested on the sands of time.

Border's genius lies in his will, in his judgment of deliveries, and in his selection of shots. Can you recall him misreading a delivery or choosing the wrong stroke? Moreover he has more shots than he imagines and plays them better, for he can hook and cut, advance down the track to thread a spinner through a gap as if he were, as one colleague wrote, threading cotton through the eye of a needle. Few men have such powers of placement.

NOR DO his extraordinary talents stop at bowling, fielding and batting. He never sought to captain Australia, played no part in the campaign which forced Kim Hughes into tearful resignation, inherited a bad team which for years had been a whipping boy and yet has managed to lead Australia to a World Cup victory, to regain and now hold the Ashes and to form a hardened outfit. And all of it without anyone thinking him an astute leader.

No doubt his selectors are wise, presumably his coach is a help, too, (though perhaps he could be quicker in correcting Steve Waugh's faults) but it has been Border on the podium throughout, dictating the tempo, surviving, shocking his men by threatening to resign every so often, occasionally folding his arms and saying, in the manner of Aneurin Bevan, 'the buggers won't work', yet finally summoning the sweetness to continue.

As captain his strength has been his disinterest in political factions, his disinterest in manipulating men and his timing, for he was too young to join World Series Cricket and was, accordingly, deemed neither a favoured son of the establishment nor a grizzled rebel. He is respected by cricketers no matter what their historical background, and no-one begrudges him the cheers which break out at his every appearance. Were it not for his evident boredom with politics, a casual observer might assume him to be supremely skilled in such affairs.

This is a man without pretension, a straightforward man who has grown from a beach boy who hated work, played cricket because it was a living and chose friends who liked a laugh into a man of stature, one who has never retreated from a fight, a captain who has by his side good blokes like Geoff Marsh and David Boon, and a captain who, being a street fighter, knew how limited-over games could be won and has gradually grasped the tactical nuances to be found in Test cricket. Because he is deliberately downbeat, he has been under-rated in every respect but his record speaks for itself and his record is that of a supremely gifted cricketer.

DEAN JONES 1

In a Calcutta orphanage a month ago I saw a 'papa' ask a child if he wanted to be a cricketer. Shyly, the boy nodded.

'You must say yes,' said the adult. 'Don't be timid. Say yes and go and do it. It is possible.'

Dean Jones used to have this impudence and it used to get him into trouble. His father had the reputation in Melbourne club cricket for being a fierce competitor who made the most of his talent. His son was just as aggressive. Jones jnr. liked to perch on the edge of the pitch, using every device to shake the batsmen.

He was prepared, he admits, to 'bend the rules a bit'. It is just as well as he has played his cricket under Allan Border's stoical leadership because Jones was a bird of prey on the field, a scavenger who expected nothing save what he could grab for himself.

He was precocious and pugnacious and his early career was dogged by impetuosity. Slim and elegant at the crease, his pinched face and straggling locks hidden under a cap, he could resemble Greg Chappell. He executed his shots with panache and his eye had a glint that mixed hardness and insolence.

Yet he flattered to deceive.

He was brilliant in miniature, a player of cameos brought down by a brashness that prevented careful thought. Just as he took command, a devil would whisper in his ear that now was the time to hit out, and, fanatically chewing gum, Jones would go for it.

He appeared to be another cricketer destined to hover on the brink.

And then Jones was dropped from the Australian team for the 1985 England tour. It was a shock to him and he reacted furiously, lashing out in State games and losing his wicket. Pretty soon his place in the Victorian XI was in peril. Critics were disappointed rather than surprised.

At this vital moment Jones had the humility to seek and to

take the advice of experienced cricketers. He consulted Ian Chappell, Bob Simpson and Keith Stackpole.

Chappell told him to begin his innings carefully, because he was too easy to get out early on.

Simpson advised him to work hard at his batting and to stop expecting the game to fall at his feet.

But it was his club colleague from Carlton, Keith Stackpole, who cut deepest. Stackpole told Jones to play each ball on its merits, irrespective of whether he'd hit 43 or 143 runs. He had lost his wicket to too many premeditated strokes, and no thoroughbred batsman could tolerate such indulgences.

Treat each ball on its merits: it's an old call and a good one.

Dean Jones had much more to give if he could conquer himself. He forced his way into the team to tour India in 1986 and in Madras defied sickness and fatigue to score 210. Every time the devils whispered in his ear he pushed singles till they left. It was, by all reports, a magnificent effort.

At last Jones was mentally as well as physically strong enough to be a class batsman. Maybe in 1985 the selectors did him a good turn.

Back home he held his position and during the next Ashes series his stocks rose. He arrived at Sydney for the fifth Test with scores of eight, 18, 27, 69, 93, two, 59 and 21.

In Sydney he constructed an unbeaten 184, an innings of majesty and command.

Strangely, his second-innings effort was hardly less impressive; his timing deserted him yet he still contributed 30 important runs. In the series he scored 511 runs at an average of 56.

Jones was now a considerable cricketer. Also, he'd settled down. Perhaps his marriage in 1986 helped in this late maturing, for, as has been frequently remarked, wedlock is an effective antidote for a man's wilder notions.

Nothing, it appeared, could go wrong.

Jones was picked as a reserve for the MCC Bicentenary game and was rated by a computer as the third best batsman around.

Then he thumped into Merv Hughes – not a course to be recommended – and crocked a knee.

The doctors shook their heads, but Jones worked ferociously hard in the gym and was back in training by autumn, defying the ugly scars that decorated his left knee.

By August he was scoring heavily in England and playing

beside great cricketers. Jones carried this form into the World Cup, clubbing the ball to leg as Australia marched to victory.

But he has not entirely mastered himself yet. Twice he lost his wicket to bad shots in Victoria's defeat at Brisbane earlier this month, shots that recalled his old, imprudent days.

Then against Tasmania he scored 191 by way of reposte, as if to remind critics that in those 10 Tests he had hit 947 runs at an average of 55.70.

Two years ago Jones' career was in ruins. Now he is captain of Victoria, married, and a respected international batsman. He has the authority to take up his mantle as a major Australian batsman.

His status will rise when he compiles regular scores in Test cricket, for regularity, not flamboyance, is the hallmark of greatness.

He can do it. It is possible.

He has been wise enough to listen to his elders and to let those devils eat their own apples.

DEAN JONES 2

Madras, Friday: As he walks out to bat in the Chepauk Stadium tomorrow afternoon, Dean Jones' spine will be tingling with the remembrance of things past.

For it was here, three years ago, that he launched his Test career by playing one of the great innings of cricket history.

Recall the circumstances. The Australians were in India for a short tour that October and had arrived in Madras to find a city sweltering in mind-numbing heat.

Only mad dogs and Englishmen went out in such weather; no-one could play cricket in it.

To acclimatise, the Australians practised hard. Extremities challenge men, Allan Border said, and it was up to them to rise to it.

Jones was not certain to play. Then Border called him to his room. An hour later Jones left ready to take on the world. It was, he says, the most inspiring talk of his career.

Play began under an unrelenting sun. So hot was it that players sitting in the pavilion carried a towel to wipe off sweat.

Outside the ground the canal was full of sewage and a distinctive odour wafted across the ground throughout the match.

Geoff Marsh was first to go, swinging wildly on 24 and leaving the field totally drained. India's wicketkeeper had already departed to hospital with a fever.

So began Jones' masterpiece.

David Boon was his first partner. Boon played back to the spinners and cut and swept when he could, while Jones darted down the pitch to drive straight.

As Shastri, Yadav and Maninder Singh asked their subtle questions, Jones talked to himself, telling himself to concentrate and do nothing rash.

Within minutes at the crease sweat was pouring off the batsmen, so much so that their boots filled with water which seeped through the lace-holes.

With grim determination Jones survived until the close, though Boon fell to the second new ball minutes earlier. After four-and-a-half rugged hours batting, Jones had scored 58.

Overnight Jones felt well, though nerves prevented him eating supper or breakfast.

He knew he had an opportunity to score a hundred and thus buy himself time to win a regular place in England that summer.

He resumed eager and fresh.

Nightwatchman Ray Bright fell for 30 or so next morning and promptly collapsed and was treated by a doctor.

Border joined Jones, master and pupil. By now lunch was approaching and Jones was feeling wobbly. Running was out of the question so the pair decided to hit singles and boundaries.

Gradually fever was taking charge of Jones and twice he urinated into his pants.

David Gilbert brought drinks out at least every three overs but Jones could keep nothing down and between balls he was vomiting.

On 160, practically in a trance, he went down to Border to say he'd had enough. Border stared into him and quietly said: 'All right, I understand. Let's get a Queenslander out here.'

Greg Ritchie was due in next.

Jones recalls: 'Once he said "Queenslander" I thought "Stuff it, I'm staying". No ruddy Queenslander was going to see me off.'

Carving mightily, Jones reached his 200 by tea on that second day.

In the interval, teammates stripped him and wrapped him in cold towels because he had not the energy to walk to the shower.

They dressed him, covered him up, and sent him back out omitting to put on his thigh pad or box.

He carried on hitting and within 20 minutes was bowled by Yadav.

Back in the pavilion physiotherapist Errol Alcott had a tub full of iced water ready for him. Alcott took his pulse and Jones 'felt real good', so good in fact that he stood up in the bath – and woke up on a saline drip in hospital.

Jones lost seven kilograms that day.

This was an innings of extraordinary courage played by a batsman whose own game is capable of swinging from Arctic snow to desert heat.

Moreover, it was a magnificent Test in which Australia declared twice and left India to score 348 on the last day. Thanks to Gavaskar and Shastri they needed one run off two balls with one wicket left.

Greg Matthews was the bowler.

A hero in his own right, he was wearing a sweater by now as if to say: 'Fellas, you ain't seen nothing yet.'

Amid great jubilation he trapped Maninder leg before and cricket had its second tie.

'No-one,' says Bobby Simpson, 'has ever been asked for more on a cricket field than was asked of Jones in Madras.'

Seldom can any batsman have experienced such a range of agony and ecstasy in so short a time.

Peter Roebuck, cricket writer of humorous bent (but serious intention).
Taunton 1986. *Patrick Eagar*

'The Godfather'. Brian Close, 2nd Test, England v West Indies, Lord's 1976. *Patrick Eagar*

The long black telegraph pole. Joel Garner, Surrey v Somerset —
County Championship — 1982. *Patrick Eagar*

The lean machine. Richard Hadlee, 1st Test, England v New Zealand, The Oval 1983. *Patrick Eagar*

White lightning. Allan Donald, Yorkshire v Warwickshire 1991. *Patrick Eagar*

Tempter of fate. David Gower, 1st Cornhill Test, England v India, Lord's 1986. *Patrick Eagar*

Bordering on the brilliant. Allan Border, Texaco One Day
International, Lord's 1989. *Patrick Eagar.*

800 million people expecting a century. Sunil Gavaskar, 2nd Test, India v England, Delhi 1984. *Patrick Eagar*

Beyond doubt a cricketing genius. Sir Garfield Sobers, 2nd Test, England v West Indies, Edgbaston 1973. *Patrick Eagar*

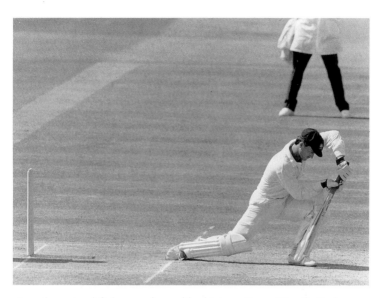

A steely-wristed fighter enchanted by history. Steve Waugh, 2nd Cornhill Test, England v Australia, Lord's 1989. *Patrick Eagar*

Robin Smith is out lbw Merv Hughes. 2nd Test, Australia v England, Melbourne 1990. *Patrick Eagar*

Etched and precise. Geoffrey Boycott, Centenary Test, England v Australia, Lord's 1980. *Patrick Eagar*

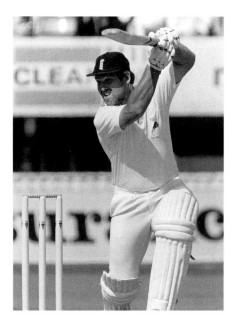

A captain of calibre.
Mike Gatting,
3rd Test, England v
India, Edgbaston 1986.
Patrick Eagar

Richards the man. Viv
Richards, Trinidad 1990.
Patrick Eagar

Absolute conviction of mastery. Viv Richards with Carl Hooper, 1st
Cornhill Test, England v West Indies, Trent Bridge 1988. *Patrick Eagar*

The archetypal Australian good bloke. Merv Hughes, 1st Cornhill Test,
England v Australia, Old Trafford 1989. *Patrick Eagar*

Slim and elegant. Dean Jones, 3rd Test, Australia v England, Adelaide 1986. *Patrick Eagar*

Botham the man. Ian Botham, 3rd Test, England v Pakistan, Headingley 1987. *Patrick Eagar*

The hottest property in cricket. Wasim Akram, 1st Cornhill Test, England v Pakistan, Old Trafford 1987. *Patrick Eagar*

Young, fit and optimistic. Waqar Younis (Surrey and Pakistan), 1990. *Patrick Eagar*

Roebuck the demon bowler. Peter Roebuck, Somerset v Middlesex, Taunton 1990. *Patrick Eagar*

Bowled Waugh. Chris Broad hits the stumps in anger. Bi-centennial Test, Australia v England, Sydney 1988. *Patrick Eagar*

STEPHEN WAUGH

Down to his bootstraps, Stephen Waugh is an Australian and a cricketer. Pinched features, durability, a contempt for fuss and a quiet sense of space speak of a gum tree in the outback. Baggy green cap pulled over the eyes even when knocking up, a splay-footed walk, a preference for patting backs when others are smacking kisses, and the fiery eyes speak of 100 years of Australian batsmen who have asked no quarter and given none.

Waugh is a steely-wristed fighter who is enchanted by history. He likes life to be simple, expects it to be tough and has no time for the shirker, a breed he contemplates as if they were a chook (a chicken) in a chook-raffle.

Without being remotely sentimental, without abandoning the national custom of irreverence, Waugh is a traditionalist. Typically, his bat is not a tree trunk, and he picks it up when the ball is delivered, which is what they did in the past and what he is going to do now. Technique interests him but he is suspicious of trends.

In the slips he is full of ideas and in the pavilion he might read about the methods of S. F. Barnes or listen to talk about Alan Kippax or Archie Jackson. To be part of this history, and to unravel cricketing skills, are his greatest desires.

Predictably, though, Stan McCabe, of the 1930s, and Doug Walters, 40 years on, are his particular heroes. He has read a biography of McCabe and has met Walters. In McCabe he must find modesty, simplicity, courage and a capacity for great deeds when the time arises.

McCabe touches the warmth in Waugh, a characteristic he otherwise hides with dry humour. In Walters he must find a man who could do it on his ear, a man who played cards, smoked cigarettes and then bashed the Poms all over the park.

With his penchant for hamburgers and mistrust of training, Waugh likes that sort of thing.

Determined to step into this tradition, and realising how many great Australian cricketers come from the bush (notably Bradman, O'Reilly and McCabe), Waugh sought the inner strength of the countryman in a harsh land, and the spontaneity of the naturally developing style.

Reared in hot, motorised, concrete Bankstown, a suburb of Sydney, Waugh dedicated himself to capturing these qualities. Keeping his own counsel, he fought his way up. It wasn't easy. Mark, his twin brother, was the stylist and many thought he'd go further.

Not so the coach of their schooldays, Harry Soloman, who sensed Stephen's fierce will. 'It was in the eyes,' he said. 'Stephen had Border's eyes, burning eyes. Stephen is hungry and the wanting is important. All champions have that quality. The eyes are cold, as if fixed on a target.'

Soloman recalled a family dinner at which cricket was discussed. Stephen sat silently fascinated. Mark was jumpy and eager to be fed. Listening to this anecdote, Mark protested: 'I was hungry,' to which Soloman smiled and chided: 'Yes, for food.' Stephen was the street fighter who, in cricket, was a man before he was a boy.

Too early, Stephen was thrust into Test cricket as an all-rounder. Times were hard. Rival states were wary of this latest great white hope from Sydney. In Australia the states heartily loathe each other; so this suspicion was trumpeted around the country.

Waugh failed in those early Tests, often the victim of poor umpiring decisions to which his reaction could be surly.

His critics pounced as if Waugh had broken a binding promise. In trouble he survived, as good men do, by living on his wits, plundering vital runs in vainglorious one-day games and bowling a cunning mixture of slow balls and yorkers to win a World Cup final.

The native intelligence of the cricketer shone through. Yet, despite this brilliance, Waugh's place in the Australian team was in jeopardy last winter, the more so when he padded up to Marshall in the first innings of the first Test. Critics were clamouring for his head and dismissing his valiant efforts for Somerset as irrelevant indulgences in third-rate cricket.

Then, like McCabe before him, Waugh decided to smash his way out of trouble. He stood up to the West Indian bombardment, gave as good as he got, bounced Viv Richards with his first three balls of the series and generally announced his intention to compete. He averaged 40 in the series.

But still he knew he wasn't a proper Test cricketer because he hadn't made a hundred. Proud to play for Australia, he felt bogus. Headingley put an end to that. Now Waugh is cock of the walk and can bat in the great tradition.

Of course, he can be stopped. Early jitters sometimes cause him to pad up to break-backs. Once set, he is formidably straight and, being a back-foot player, late in defence. His aggressive shots offer hope because they are played on the up and with an open face. Certainly on hard Australian pitches the West Indian slip cordon didn't dare neglect its duty.

Nevertheless, he started hitting hundreds, started thinking as a batsman rather than as an all-rounder and can be expected to impose himself as a daring, combative and essentially correct batsman.

GOWER

As David Gower packed his bags in preparation for The Oval, a patrician voice in a Hampshire dressing room called out: 'For God's sake, David, get a big one.'

It was meant well. Gower engages hearts rather than heads and hearts were crying out. Gower's response was surprisingly snappy for so wistful a man. He had detected a strain of patronage in the remark and said so. Only so often can a man tolerate being told to pull up his socks.

We have all done it. Worrying about Gower is a national pastime. If only, we sigh, if only he'd knuckle down, he'd score heaps of runs. If only he'd play straight, move his feet, concentrate, stop fiddling and flicking, we could watch him without fearing a seizure.

Gower is a seductive cricketer. Because of his appearance – handsome, diffident and apparently doomed – and his style, with its hint of charabanc, cane and top hat, he is cast as a romantic hero.

Half England wants to mother him or marry him, and everyone else wants to bat as he does, as if in some enchanted dream. Wry in calamity, nonchalant in triumph, never straining too hard, Gower carries his followers with him wherever he goes, on a journey without malice which might bring immense joy.

Accordingly, when David last Tuesday rose to slay his Goliath, thousands stood to cheer him, and even hardened men, they say, felt lumps in their throats.

Truly, we like to see a pleasant fellow, stoical in adversity, survive. We like our cavaliers, and yet there is more to it than that. An illusion has been created: Gower as a fragile genius in a rough world; Gower as a man who could be great were he tough enough.

Years ago, I said he was content to be a minor genius. I was wrong. He just *is* a minor genius. One thing above all was obvious from his effort last week. He is a gritty, resilient cricketer who can summon a masterpiece every so often, but commonly can play only minor pieces which are a delight in their expression and a frustration in their want of intellectual rigour.

Gower, like everyone else, scores as many runs as he deserves to score, as many as he is capable of scoring, for to do otherwise is to be otherwise, and this is beyond him. Was Strauss chastised for failing to write symphonies?

Gower is not some delicate creature in need of bucking up. His contemporaries, Gooch, Lamb, Botham and Gatting, have suffered sharper swings of fortune save as captains, an area in which Gower is plainly inadequate, for he cannot communicate fight.

Gooch, in particular, has endured lean spells, and not so long ago, for he seeks to be master of his own fate and is nonplussed, sometimes to the point of panic, when it cannot be so. Lacking analytical powers, and more relaxed, Gower is willing to allow cricket to follow its majestic course and to absorb its blows. Gooch dictates. Gower accepts. Gooch wants to destroy bowlers; Gower plays cricket with them.

Moreover, Gower is a conscientious cricketer, seldom missing a game, never leaving the field for a smoke and rarely carrying a pound of excess baggage. Throughout his career, he has batted in the top four, where it hurts. His ambition, his drive, shone through at The Oval even to those of us hitherto reluctant to see it, those who mistook diffidence for complacency.

When he fails it is, as with most players, due to an error of judgment, a fault of technique or a good delivery. It is not a matter of knuckling down. In his terms he already is knuckling down, already is everything he can be.

For years they wanted Boycott to be more like Gower. Now they want Gower to be more like Boycott.

But wait. Does not Gower thrive in Test cricket and fail for his county, and is this evidence of a lazy genius? Not so. Ken Barrington averaged 58 for England and 54 for Surrey and no one ever accused him of being lacklustre.

As an impressionist, Gower bats as if in a blur. No mathematician he, for lines and lengths are not easily distinguished, and he relies upon arm and wrist to avoid trouble. Sometimes this fails, and he is out to apparently wishy-washy shots, while others stand and stare upon being dismissed, as if undone by a snorter.

Test cricket suits Gower. Test pitches are often hard and flat, so that his hands can save him from his feet's neglect. Fast bowlers hold no terrors for him, especially if they do not move the ball unduly.

Fields tend to be aggressive (they were astonishingly so at The Oval), and this helps Gower, too, for his backlift is sketchy and forces him to chip his shots, especially to leg, where men are rarely stationed in five-day matches.

David will go to Australia as a battle-hardened Test cricketer, a player at his best, a man who cannot change and a man entirely capable of taking care of himself.

ROBIN SMITH

Robin Smith arrived in Australia with a fearsome reputation as a batsman capable of committing assault and battery upon all sorts of bowlers, a reputation apparently confirmed with aggressive innings of 41, 98 not out, 71 and 58 not out in the preparatory games. But now Smith is suffering a decline as painful as any endured by a distinguished England batsman here since Denis Compton scored 53 runs in seven Test innings 40 years ago.

In three Tests this summer Smith has hit 74 runs at an average of 14.8, and in eight limited-over innings he has managed 104 runs, a dismal sequence and one to remind cricketers everywhere of how fickle is this game, a game which constantly asserts its mastery over humble players, a game in which, sometimes, there is no second chance – merely a long and lonely walk back to the pavilion, energy all unspent.

In cricket, a batsman can slide from bad to worse with terrible alacrity. Upon taking guard, a struggling fellow sees fieldsmen with biceps like meat pies crowding around him, a gap nowhere to be found; moreover his bat is the wrong weight, his boots are heavy, the light is grim and the pitch suddenly green. Scenting blood, opposing bowlers charge in, for they have suffered, too, while umpires, sensing doubt, find their fingers itching as if eager to put the wretch out of his misery.

And so it goes on, as it is with Smith right now. Australia have bowled well to him, much better than in 1989 when their approach was bullish, when they fed his rasping square cut just one of which could set his pulse racing now, restoring remembrance of deeds past, of a summer two years ago when he hit 553 runs against these very opponents, of a season recently finished when he took 361 runs for twice out off India.

To see Smith walking out to bat this month has been to see a man desperately trying to recapture a mood, for he marches out as before, determined to assert himself physically, swinging his arms as aggressively as a boxer entering a ring, a Tyson not a

Fenech, for he has never been a subtle sportsman, relies on power rather than touch. This is a man bent upon dictating his fates who finds himself swallowed up by them, utterly unable to resist their cruel appetites. Smith likes to feel confident, in charge. He is a batsman who bristles or dies.

And herein lies Smith's difficulty. His game is all belligerence, as Dean Jones is all daring. Yet he is not a belligerent fellow, not at all, rather an old-fashioned sporting type, one who married a Hampshire girl, enjoys fishing, shooting and drinking in his local pub The Three Tuns (just one would do for now). He lacks the inner swagger predicted by his style, is a batsman who seldom feels as masterly as he appears.

Accordingly, he suffers periods of doubt during which emerges a caricature, a batsman urgently thrusting his pad forward, for he must do something, must be decisive, a move which cramps his shots square of the wicket, shots which are overwhelmingly his strength. By instinct, he must get close to the ball, especially when he is on edge for his triumphs have not been won by craft or submission. Yet technically, he needs to be a distance from the ball to execute his shots with their customary conclusive freedom, is a distance away when he is playing well, though memory may not say so. Out of sorts, Smith's technique and temperament are in conflict.

Everyone is trying to help, for England have sore need of his runs. During the Melbourne Test Geoff Boycott was to be seen on the square giving his counsel. Showing how to play Bruce Reid by hitting him towards mid-on. Chris, his brother and an accomplished batting colleague at Hampshire, has also been in the nets offering fraternal assistance. No doubt Robin has listened carefully, partly because he is dutiful and polite, partly because he lacks Gower's resistance to change. No doubt he is trying to put their wise words into practice for, though he will not show it, failure is hitting hard.

And yet I wonder if this intensity, this depth of analysis is a help or a hindrance.

To my mind, tension, not technique, lie at the core of Smith's failures, though of course sheer bad luck has played its part. Being a brave fellow, his standards are high and once he did not live up to them, in Brisbane, he began to wonder if something was wrong and to seek correction. But nothing really was wrong, or nothing which a few bold drives could not put right. Rather

Smith had put himself under formidable pressure, as do men who expect themselves to succeed and are playing in a losing side. Rather than seek salvation in method Smith could trust his competitive instincts, which have served him well until now.

MATCH REPORTS

AUSTRALIA VERSUS ENGLAND

Second Test at Perth, November 1986

Wɪᴛʜ his score on 114 Jack Richards received a full toss from Chris Matthews and hit it to the boundary. A spectator called out, 'Hey, that's friendly, Chris, real friendly.'

So it was throughout the day. So it has been since Friday morning. The Australian bowling has been breathtakingly incompetent and for the seventh time in the last eight Test matches against Australia, England have scored more than 450.

Rarely, even in India, can a team have batted for two days with so little trouble. Not even Bob Hawke could do anything about it. He did try. Immediately upon his arrival in the press box Botham was out, flicking at a wide one. 'Got him,' yelled Australia's Prime Minister. 'You beauty . . . Well done, Reidy . . . There's your story, fellows.'

Hawke left two minutes later, at 12.18, and Australia did not take another wicket for 215 minutes, in which time David Gower and Richards scored 217 runs. By the end of their partnership these two were treating the Australian bowling with a disdain bordering on contempt.

Gower smacked a short ball from Lawson back over his head and Richards stepped back to guide an off-spinner through cover. There was not much Border could do. His fast men, so shoddy on Friday, did manage to hold England for an hour and a half in the morning and did take the wickets of Gatting, slicing a drive to cover, Broad, out of position as he tried to force off the back foot, and Botham.

For 90 minutes the bowling was not too dreadful. After that the Australians were torn to pieces by an extremely good batsman and by a useful one.

Jack Richards can bat a bit. He scored 1,000 runs for Surrey last year and he has a cunning way of working the ball through gully. He is not a player of a high calibre, just a steady professional, the sort Test bowlers ought to be able at least to contain.

In Perth yesterday he could scarcely believe his luck as he belted the ball around the field as if he were Viv, not Jack. He reached his 100 in 195 minutes off 168 balls, very few of which troubled him. He did not offer a sniff of a chance, not even as he improvised as Gatting prepared to declare.

He batted well, but when Richards is able to treat a nation's bowling in this way, it is time to go back to the drawing-board. Eventually he was caught in the deep to end an intrepid innings which was a revelation to his friends and a scourge to the Australians.

Gower is, of course, an accomplished player. He was at his best in this innings, reaching his 100 off 125 balls. At the crease he drifted back to persuade the ball to the off and he punctuated his innings with graceful drives which brought gasps from the crowd.

Watching Gower bat is one of life's pleasures. Occasionally he was imprecise in the execution of his strokes. But for the most part he was elegant and effective. He scored many of his runs with pulls and back-drives from balls that were not short. By the time he was out, lobbing a catch, the Australians were in a daze, undone this time not by brutality but by kindness.

Australia missed their chance on Friday when the pitch was fresh. For an hour scarcely a ball was bowled at the stumps, and wicketkeeper Zoehrer flung himself around to collect the new ball wasted by the bowlers.

Chris Matthews, so raw that he has neither a regular run nor a grooved action, was the worst offender: he is untutored yet to be the hope of the nation. Reid bowled with purpose and was never taken lightly; still, he is only a fair bowler who was, after all, bowling to Jack Richards and England did score 592 runs.

Lawson was disappointing, the slowest of this amiable trio. He was a shadow of the man who took 32 wickets in the 1982–83 series and may be near the end of his career.

Nor did the support bowlers offer much. Waugh is military medium and probably doesn't consider himself to be a bowler. Greg Matthews dragged his off-spinners too wide of the stumps to be effective.

Really this was scarcely a county attack let alone a Test attack. None of the bowlers presented problems once the shine was gone. There were no subtleties or deceits or riddles to be unravelled. They were plodding and pedestrian.

Not that this is really an Australian attack at all, simply an inferior version of an English one. Four seamers and a finger spinner were chosen as if this were a damp pitch in Derby.

On this rock-hard surface batsmen must be beaten in the air, with swing or flight, or off the pitch by bowlers who cut the ball by ripping their fingers across it, or spin it by snapping their wrist. These Australians relied too much on swing and once it was gone so were their prospects.

Without pace or wrist-spin or cut, a moderate batting side would score runs on such a pitch. Yet, on the morning of the match, with a white pitch and under a hot sun, the selectors left out their leg-spinner, Peter Sleep. There are three leg-spinners on the selection panel, including Bob Simpson, the manager.

Australian teams used to pick two fast bowlers, a leg-spinner and a left-arm spinner. Men who merely hit the seam were regarded as cannon-fodder. Moreover, English batsmen worry about leg-spinners. Despite this, Border was given a modest attack from which his one bowler capable of surprise was omitted. Macbeth murdered Sleep; maybe they feared Gatting might do the same.

Until Border is given a proper Australian attack it is idle to imagine he can lead his team to victory. Until an Australian team is chosen to play Australian cricket it is hard to see any hope for the home team.

This is not to belittle the efforts of Gower or Richards, let alone those of Broad and Athey. Though he never got into his stride yesterday, Broad's innings was impressive. He tucked the ball to leg and punched it smoothly off the back foot past point. He even essayed a square cut, a cross-bat shot from a straight bat player. By and large, though, he did not do anything too exotic. He is phlegmatic and ambitious, as his move from Bristol to Trent Bridge testified. He played within his limitations and intends to open for England for some time.

And Athey was not on song; he was dropped three times and twice awoke the umpire. His hooking was sketchy and if he is to be solid in defence he must cut out these forays into the unknown.

Sadly, enjoyable as was the stroke-play of Gower and Broad, the first two days of the match were dominated by the inadequacies of the Australian bowling. This is the same England team that left Heathrow on October 9. Jack Richards is the fellow who keeps wicket for Surrey. They are not suddenly supermen. They are encountering some woeful Australian bowling.

Border's men might save this game, though. Late in the day, Matthews turned one enough to elude Zoehrer. Edmonds and Emburey, with a huge total to help them, will harass the batsmen into mistakes. Maybe the cracks will widen, too, adding uneven bounce to the difficulties of the Australians. If they do lose, the Australians may as well go back to that drawing-board and might just as well select an old-fashioned team which would, at least, stretch the batsmen.

AUSTRALIA VERSUS ENGLAND

Bicentenary Test at Sydney, January 1988

On Tuesday majestic old ships sailed into Sydney harbour. Hundreds of yobs followed in their wake.

And the shore was packed with picnickers enjoying the re-enactment and waiting for nightfall to see the fireworks over the bridge. Into this heady atmosphere arrived an embattled and weakened England team full of competent professionals determined to build their careers.

England's majestic ships were in dry dock – Gower on safari, Gooch by his fireside, Lamb in the Orange Free State, and Botham at the SCG bar – and the remainder reacted like Muslims at a Christmas party: observing the festivities, thinking them a lot of rot and going quietly about their business. Maybe it was a mistake to arrange a Test match to recognise a non-cricketing occasion. Test cricketers rarely react like performing seals to the demands of a crowd.

And fortunately the only cricketing firework evident during the first two days came from Chris Broad who, upon losing his wicket, knocked over a stump. He was facing Stephen Waugh who, in an effort to shake a stubborn opponent, had been pounding a few lively bouncers, all of which Broad had ducked.

Waugh tried another bouncer. Broad saw it and prepared to move under it. To his dismay the ball did not rise. Broad froze. The ball hit him on the elbow and ricocheted into his wicket. He turned and smashed at his stumps before leaving the field with acerbic remarks ringing in his ears and to the boos of the crowd.

On his walk back Broad thumped his helmet with his bat as he realised the stupidity of his conduct and the certainty of his finding himself in hot water. In the stand eminent authorities, notably Raman Subba Row, Peter May, Colin Cowdrey and

J. J. Warr observed his deed. He could expect no sympathy and Peter Lush quickly announced that Broad had been fined £500.

Some consider this unduly lenient. In mitigation Broad had batted in scorching heat for 7½ hours, without ever finding his timing, frequently misjudging McDermott's slower ball, frequently edging his cuts over slip. By his standards it was not a secure innings. Beyond doubt he was exhausted and restrained. Besides which he was not questioning a decision, could not do so having been bowled.

None of this remotely excuses his conduct which was foolish and headstrong. If he offends again he can expect to be dropped which would be a pity because he is a dedicated if ambitious cricketer whose worst enemy is himself.

Apart from this unhappy drama the game moved along as a backcloth to the parades, anthems, songs and handshakes, a game crying out for someone to take it by the scruff of the neck. Nobody could do so as England's batsmen failed to forge an aggressive partnership, an unsurprising failure in a team including so many opening batsmen and tailenders.

This is a scratch England team and it played like it, the batsmen defending solidly and attacking fitfully, losing their wickets in predictable ways, Moxon because his footwork was leaden, Robinson edging a short ball to slip and Athey having a rush of blood.

Of those capable of imposing themselves, Gatting could find only one hook before being beaten by a leg-cutter from Waugh and Capel lifted his head against Taylor after playing several forthright if unproductive shots. He is a lively cricketer with an optimism indicating calibre.

Things did brighten up down the order as French, Foster and Emburey took toll of an attack deadened by hours of thankless work. French swept as busily if not yet quite so infuriatingly as Knott, and Emburey played a range of low-brow shots to good effect whereupon Foster hit hard. All fell in the late charge in anticipation of a declaration. Overall it was an uneasy performance that spoke of unfamiliarity and of the friendliness of the preparation in New Zealand.

Australia's preparation for this game was worse, embracing 10 one-day matches. Only Peter Sleep, dropped from the one-day squad, has played a sensible game since the turn of the year. With Bruce Reid injured and Craig McDermott hampered by a wonky knee, Border's bowling was threadbare. Though both Taylor and Sleep took wickets they bowled too many bad deliveries. Of Taylor's four wickets Athey was caught as he danced down the pitch, Capel swiped, French tried a hit over cover and Foster edged a drive to slip.

Sleep did turn the ball to beat Emburey but he was too inaccurate for Border to set an aggressive field. After Abdul Qadir he must have been a blessed relief. Dodemaide was accurate and persevering, but only Waugh served up stuff appropriate for a Test match.

To add to their woes Australia dropped several catches, the most culpable yesterday being Marsh's miss of French at point and Dyer's dropping of Emburey off Dodemaide. No wonder Border appeared lethargic at slip. Maybe he considers this celebration to be a bridge too far after a hard season that began in India four months ago.

On the road ever since, he let this game drift by, changing his bowlers when he had to, using McDermott and Dodemaide in long spells, practically ignoring Waugh after lunch on both days, and sending Taylor to the boundary to reflect upon his full tosses and misfields. Border has captained well this year and his team has improved, but on the evidence of these two days you'd never have guessed it.

Whatever happens this will not be a good Bicentenary game. One team is nervous, the other is tired and both are finding the occasion artificial. Perhaps it is just as well that, as one local put it, 'These games only happen every 20 years.'

A DAY TO WIN,
A DAY TO CELEBRATE,
A DAY TO REMEMBER

Awakening at 8am I make some toast and watch a Bertie Wooster video. Need cheering up after 14 days on the field and nights on the road.

Dog tired, of course, but so, hopefully, is everyone else.

Down to the ground to have a net, a warm-up, a peer at the wicket and to shake hands with sponsors. We want to bat first because it is a muggy day and the ball might swing. Tavaré always wins the toss. He loses it.

March out with Cook at 11 am, trying to appear combative. Cook goes early, nibbling around off-stump on a pitch surprisingly dead in its bounce. I reach 17, feeling good, light on my toes, the acid test.

Facing Cowans, a line and length merchant these days, impeccably accurate after his wild years. Bit like Henry IV, really. Gatting moves a man across to cover, leaving a gap at mid-on. Temptation.

I try for it and am beaten as Cowans cuts one back. Might have kept a little low too. Bad shot, though, out of position and couldn't adjust.

Poor concentration. They say it gets harder as years go by. Boycott seemed to manage all right.

Could have scored 100 really. When will I ever learn? Does anyone ever learn anything?

Back to glum dressing room. Two important men already gone and only 35 scored.

They had expected me to do well, I could sense it. Been lucky on big occasions in the past. Take pads off and have a nap.

Not really sleeping, just dozing, lost in thought. Then potter around the ground, signing benefit books, saying hello to people. No good at sitting on balconies and watching. Talk too much.

Somerset stutter along until lunch, losing wickets just as the tide has turned.

Sleep for the rest of the innings, sluggish and weary. Awaken to find Somerset all out for 183. Not enough, of course.

Perhaps we had set our sights too high. Pressed too early. So many vast scores at Taunton these days and we assumed we needed 270, made mistakes and failed to reach 230.

But low scores can be dangerous, because chasing them seems such a formality.

Desmond Haynes launches the Middlesex reply. Right forward and right back, dropping at his toes and running. He is very impressive, probably the best one-day player in the world, though Dean Jones might not agree.

Haynes cuts loose at Adrian Jones, our puffing fast bowler whose game is all aggression. Three sizzling boundaries culminating in a flamboyant drive through point. Haynes holds his position for a few seconds, playing to his gallery.

Enraptured, he waves to his colleagues; Ramprakash waves back, flicking his wrist in Caribbean celebration.

Two balls later, adrenalin pumping, Haynes is out, caught at mid-on by yours truly; bit of a relief really. I haven't caught so well lately.

We had been at his mercy. Gatting appears and is booed. Confused fellow. Suspicious of intellectuals, yet every intellectual I have met with an opinion on the matter strongly supported his England captaincy.

He takes ages to break his duck, then cuts loose at Rose, formerly a colleague, whom he may consider a bit soft. Sixteen off the over. And then Gatting, too, is gone, bowled by 'Tulip' Lefebvre, who is rising to the occasion. Yesterday, Lefebvre was military medium. Now he is fizzing.

Careless of Middlesex to lose two wickets but this is a game of careless batting. At tea, it is their match, 85 for two, wickets and time to spare. Taunton is like a morgue.

Jimmy Cook thinks they are too confident and says: 'No game is over till the fat lady comes,' an obscure and not entirely verbatim phrase of clear enough meaning.

He thinks Roseberry will run himself out. Within an over he does so, wasting a wicket on a gamble.

A few overs later, unbelievably, a second run out, as Ramprakash, whose manner upsets those of democratic persuasion, calls for a single and Tavaré swoops, if ageing warriors can swoop, turns and throws down the stumps.

Tavaré raises his hands in elation. Never seen such animation from him before, anywhere. They are 100 for four. Not a crisis, but interesting. Taunton is getting noisy.

Mallender is summoned and Ramprakash is trapped in front: 122 for five. Butcher and Downton, old campaigners both, edge forwards, taking singles. They need 45 in 11 overs and have five wickets in hand. It is almost too easy.

They try to advance stealthily, pinching runs and avoiding risks. Perhaps they are too cautious. Chasing a stiffer target is easier sometimes, as it allows belligerence. In this hour, Tavaré calls me up.

Vic Marks used to do that. It is easier for occasionals sometimes because we have nothing to lose. Slow pitch, turning a bit now, just bowl straight and give nothing away. Above all, don't do anything clever. Can't anyhow.

Adrian Jones is bowling too, all red face and wild eyes, like a bull who has run a marathon. It is 6.45 pm. Hours have flashed by, and overs are trickling by. The scoreboard says they must win, yet the mood is different. There is a game on.

Butcher hooks at Jones and miscues to long-leg. Guess who is at long-leg? Up and up it goes, up and up, three miles at least.

I have time to peer around to see if any colleague is interested in having a stab at it. Not a man moves. Unavoidably it is mine. It is over my head. No it isn't, it is a yard in front, I think.

It falls and I reach forward, catching it an inch from the turf, appearing nonchalant and feeling white. Pure luck, really. Bedlam in the ground, loudest noise since 1979, happy days. 144 for six.

Williams enters and swipes. A big appeal and a finger goes up to herald another roar. 150 for seven. They still need 34 and it must seem like a mountain to them. Jones steams in, and traps Downton in front, no argument about the decision. 153 for eight.

Incredibly, only Emburey and the tail are left. I bowl to Simon Hughes, further appeals rend the air. He is caught between hitting and batting responsibly.

I am worried about my trousers. You have to cover up everything these days. It is a bit like Watergate. I've lent my plaster to Hayhurst who found himself wearing the wrong shirt. The maker's name can be seen on my trousers.

Lord's will be watching on BSB I suppose, if they've got it. Presumably someone has it. I might get fined, and then I think the hell with it. It is only a minute or two.

Hughes swings, misses and is bowled. Cowans enters, swings and is bowled by Jones. It is all over. A shout of incredulous delight, a shout heard all over town, rends the air. A rush to the dressing room and a feeling of rare exhiliration. Middlesex had blinked and lost.

It was a wonderful fight-back. Probably Somerset's best limited-over victory in a decade. Champagne in dressing room. I have a bath and go to a meeting about my benefit. Then I join the celebrations.

Hours later a colleague approaches and says: 'Christ, Roebuck, you're a difficult man.' It was a compliment, I think.

MCG CLASH DOWN TO A
TEST OF NERVE

PRESSURE is such a potent factor in Test cricket.

In its grip, Chris Matthews once sprayed his deliveries as if he were firing flak at a squadron of bombers. Under its spell, Steve Waugh, fresh from a devastating hand in Perth, missed a goodish one and was bowled, adding to his worries. Time and again he has risen to the challenge of a tight finish in front of a vast crowd, yet he can fall when the pressure is personal rather than collective.

Tension has been at the heart of events in this thrilling Test match from the start. So edgy was David Gower in the hours before play began that he turned upon a trespassing photographer with uncharacteristic anger, so ridding himself of much frustration. A day later, nerves excited, he contributed a spell-binding yet scarcely immaculate 100.

Allan Border is another who can be testy, even grumpy, as he steels himself for battle, a period when men would be private and yet must be public. But repeatedly he has summoned every power at his disposal to construct important innings, as he did yester-day. During England's innings he had not been in his most festive mood, standing hand on hip like a teapot, feeling betrayed by every edge that brought no wicket, begrudging every run.

Plainly, he thrives upon tension because it is not as if he is obviously a genius, for his supremacy over other men consists rather in the perfection of those qualities he pre-eminently pos-sesses than in their variety or extent. Quite simply, he has a rigorous technique, one tried and tested against every bowler, one that has endured like a rock pounded by furious seas.

All summer, Australia has applied unrelenting pressure upon its opponents, running superbly, catching flies and pushing their foes backwards until they began to doubt their own prowess.

Yesterday, at last, it was the England players' turn to apply pressure, and they did so magnificently, with bowling of telling accuracy. It was bowling that denied easy runs, that stopped batsmen used to airing dazzling shots from scoring at above two an over.

Accordingly, whenever Australia appeared certain to take command it was turned back, not least by Mark Taylor and Dean Jones, whose efforts to play major innings calculated to determine the outcome of this game and this series, was restrained. Had the tourists lost control, they might as well have packed their bags and headed for home.

They did not do so, not for a second; rather they played hard Test cricket, applying a plan devised to deny Australia's aggressive intent. Graham Gooch, an inspiring captain, won from his men conviction, concentration and effort, a combination that allowed them to break through at vital times, to strike whenever Australia wavered, which they did twice after a drinks break.

Gooch's tactic of asking bowlers to cramp Australia's premier batsmen, both left-handers, by bowling around the wicket worked so splendidly that Border and Taylor scored 123 runs in their 485 minutes in occupation.

Angus Fraser, of course, was England's particular hero, bowling long spells – too long it seemed at times – and maintaining an unremitting length, flogging his legs as he ran in and plodding back to his mark as if he could barely reach it. Here was valour as impressive as Bruce Reid's effort on hot Wednesday, as admirable as Merv Hughes in Perth two seasons ago.

Fraser hardly moved a ball in the air, was constantly facing aggressive and confident batsmen and yet managed to restore English hopes by taking 6/34 in 26 overs of unremitting effort. He simply would not give up, and nor would his colleagues as they fought to stop Australia securing a lead. No wonder teammates shook his hand as he walked off.

Fraser is a fine bowler but he needed support and was given it by Devon Malcolm, who hardly strayed to leg and was capable of reminding batsmen of his presence by directing one at their scones. If the pitch cracks up he could be a handful.

Nor did DeFreitas or Tufnell disappoint, though Tufnell found himself asked to bowl outside leg stump to Dean Jones during England's solitary unsatisfactory period. Jones is a dangerous player who unsettles every bowler, but he had not taken charge yet and Tufnell may be too inexperienced to use such a strategy.

Nevertheless, this was a day that held every spectator in its thrall, one upon which Australia's efforts to take charge were constantly denied. Pressure forced Border's men into mistakes, for this pitch was uneven and they were given nothing to hit. Accordingly, this match remains to be decided. An atmosphere of something about to happen has been evident throughout, and time alone will tell if it is to fade away or erupt into life.

So far neither team, nor any individual, has dictated for any length of time, no sudden tumble of wickets has occurred and no aggressive innings have been sustained. No doubt both teams returned to their rooms exhausted and exhilarated last night, and much will depend upon whose nerve holds longest today. This was Test cricket at its very best and yet only 197 runs were scored.

TEMPTER OF FATE

Something strange happened in Melbourne yesterday.

A batsman was poised on 98 and searching for the two runs that would convert an innings of humble origin into one of rich maturity. Since the pitch was as whey-faced as a powdered actress, and since the batsman was playing particularly well, such an advance appeared certain.

Yet he was on edge, a tension shared by 20,735 spectators, all glued to their seats and willing this fellow to his hundred. Gasps greeted every hint of danger and a man yelled 'no' as a loud appeal rent the air. Perilously close it was, but the umpire did his duty and shook his head.

An off-drive was played and throaty cheers suppressed as cover prevented a second run. Finally, a ball was nudged to mid-wicket and at once spectators stood to cheer, a reaction acknowledged with a modest raising of the bat. Joy and relief were evident in every face.

Target reached, concentration wavered and a return catch was lifted, whereupon this fellow wandered dreamily off to a second loud reception.

And this fellow is an Englishman! David Gower's popularity in Australia is itself a phenomenon. Here is a man as blue-blooded as Douglas Jardine, a leisurely fellow who never courts popularity, never seeks elevation to the temporary rank of folk hero. Yet wherever he goes he is greeted with a warmth usually reserved for the return of a long-lost friend.

In Brisbane, he was awarded an astonishing ovation, one that surprised, moved and inspired him, and Melbourne was just as generous. Like Kim Hughes, whom he in some ways resembles, Gower is more honoured here than on his own patch.

Gower worries England, a land after all in which a Puritan once led a popular revolution. Educators have taken charge of games and transformed them, more or less, into a cross-country run followed by a cold shower on the principle that if it does not hurt it cannot be much good. Gower is not much of a chap for cold showers and will go cross-country only if accompanied by a jeep, a camera, a crate of champagne and several flamingoes. Accordingly, when he fails, the Puritans sigh and say: 'If only the confounded fellow would put his head down.'

Gower is never anguished, never changes his style and is less productive in domestic cricket than is indicated by his Test record, his failures due to a style more suited to flat pitches and open spaces than to medium pace and movement, the lot of a regular county batsman.

Australia rarely sees these failures, sees Gower only in his element, playing tantalising innings in Test matches. Spectators see superlative cover drives, two of which were aired in Melbourne yesterday, two flowing strokes off Alderman, as smooth as a breeze across a prairie. Another flick of the wrist sent a ball directed at his hips speeding on its way, a shot of class.

If Gower is enchanting he is also flirtatious and every ball has a life of its own, a life full of possibilities, for Gower's reaction cannot be predicted, especially by himself. He plays by eye, by instinct, not by method and believes he must stay true to this for has it not served him well over the years?

Ever flitting on the edge of danger, he can suddenly suffer a burst of recklessness as he did against Reid on Wednesday, walking away from his crease as if to disown one especially wanton shot and promptly playing a worse one next ball. Girls want to marry him, ladies want to mother him, stuffed shirts want to thrash him and everyone wishes they could bat like he does when his luck is in.

To top it off, he is a friendly fellow untarnished by aggressive posturing, a fellow who plays with, as much as against, his opponents, and treats cricket as a game. Australians appreciate his spontaneity and can see, too, that he knows what it is to lose, and can feel sympathy, for men such as this are not supposed to lose and yet must do so, most of the time.

Finally, Gower does not prevaricate, gets on with the job in a manner traditionally treasured by spectators here who value aggressive skills above all. It is a part of the English temperament to develop a defensive strategy to win games, to reduce and to confine, all of which irritates people here.

Gower may never be quite as appreciated in England, for unlike other distinguished players he cannot transform a losing side. Supporters want him to challenge fate, yet he accepts it, however bad. Upon the clean-bowled first ball in Ballarat, he simply smiled and walked off, just as he did yesterday.

Doubtless, these astonishingly touching receptions will continue. After all, Australia has a couple of useful left-handers of its own, and a winning team to boot.

APARTHEID AND
OTHER ISSUES

TIME TO BITE THE SOUTH AFRICAN BULLET

For the first time the ICC has produced a cut and dried position on South Africa. Finally England has abandoned its insistence upon the rights of county cricketers to go there in the winter. Though this position was reached by pragmatism rather than principle I support it.

I do not support it because it will hold cricket together – it may fail to do this – but because at last cricket is standing firm against apartheid. Cricket is a non-racial game and should have no truck with racism.

Apartheid can be funny. A decade ago white Eddie Barlow and black Lawrence Rowe were playing for Derbyshire. Rowe was grizzling that he couldn't find a gardener. Finally Barlow exploded. He'd had enough. 'At home, boy, you'd do the bloody garden,' he bellowed.

It has its horrifying side too. Recently Eric Sambo accidentally ran over and killed Jacobus Vorster's dog. Sambo was a black servant, Vorster his white master. Vorster tied Sambo to a tree and beat him to death. In court Vorster was fined 3,000 rand and given a five-year suspended sentence. This was in South Africa.

A few days ago John Carlisle and Norris McWhirter were in court too, arguing about principles. They spoke in high-falutin terms about freedom. It's a pity that they don't set equality of races as high as the freedom of 300 county cricketers. Can the right of players to go where they like stand aside the right of races to be equal?

If Malcolm Marshall had been born in South Africa he'd be inferior and not allowed a significant vote. This is the freedom that matters. Beside it all others pale into insignificance.

Other tales can be told. Valence Watson was a good rugby player but he was also a man of conscience, a damned nuisance in fact. He began playing rugby for black teams. Vengeful authority banned him for life. Later he was dishonourably discharged from the army for refusing to sanction the brutalisation of blacks.

Later still, the clothes shop he'd opened in a township was burnt down. Watson was charged with arson; they said he needed the insurance money. The state's only witness complained of police brutality. His original evidence was believed. Defence witnesses were ignored and Watson was sent to jail for 30 months. So are the courageous rewarded where only the whites are free.

And let not the advocates of sporting freedom trail the red herring about prejudice in the West Indies. Two of the West Indian selectors (Hendricks and Carew) are of mixed descent. The presidents of the cricketing bodies in Trinidad and Barbados are variously Chinese and British. One of the four Barbadian selectors is white. Fully 75 per cent of the West Indian population is African, yet eight of the players in the first Red Stripe Shield game in the West Indies were non-African.

Comparisons with apartheid are pathetic attempts to tar everyone else with the same brush.

Nor are the works of Ali Bacher relevant. Beyond argument Bacher has worked prodigiously hard to bring cricket to thousands of impoverished and dispossessed black children. Already three youngsters – Walter Masemola, Billy Mabena and Gift Marthe – are playing for the Transvaal under-age team. This is a magnificent effort but the kids are still impoverished and dispossessed. It is political freedom, not sporting freedom, that is the debate.

Predictably, English cricketers are up in arms, standing by their right to choose. It is up to the employers to find alternative jobs, a task they have neglected in the past. But however much sympathy one has for the plight of these cricketers it pales beside the victims in foreign jails.

Some people, notably Jack Bannister, are predicting rebel tours. Bannister's contribution is disturbing. He is secretary of the players' association. He is predicting, if not advocating, rebel tours. He also works for South African television so his independence is open to question. It is not fit that the secretary of the players' association is so closely tied to South African interests.

Players can still go to South Africa. It is up to them. If they go they must be prepared to pay the price. Rumour has it that some Test cricketers will be going. Probably they do not contemplate next winter's trip to the West Indies with equanimity. It would help the boycott if Test cricket and winter tours could be better organised.

Cricket is by no means in order but January's meeting was a step forward. Only when apartheid is abolished will either cricketers or South African blacks be happy. County cricketers must bite this bullet and accept their responsibility in the war against racism. All efforts should be made to stop players going. England would be best served by those keenest to play.

THE CARROT

This morning the professional cricketers of England gather in Birmingham for what could be their most contentious meeting since Packer. Top of the agenda is the International Cricket Conference ban on those who coach or play in South Africa after April 1, 1989. So important is the meeting that all the leading protagonists have accepted invitations to speak.

The Cricketers' Association's position is simple. While reluctantly acknowledging the need for a playing ban to preserve Test cricket, upon which county finances depend, they argue that coaching trips should be permitted. The Test and County Cricket Board insists that no such compromise is possible.

Ali Bacher, representing the official South African line, will side with the association by saying that they are coaching thousands of children in black townships. It's an old tune which sceptics have been hearing from South Africa since 1970. To date, stories about multi-racial cricket have been claptrap. Now there is something in it, a scraping of the surface. Both sides appear to want settlement rather than battle.

Last month I went to South Africa to see what Bacher was doing. Besides Bacher, I spoke to the African National Congress and attended sundry radical meetings. Though still hating apartheid, still backing the boycott, I concluded that the coaches were doing splendid work.

Alexandra, like Soweto, is a sprawling, degrading, black township on the fringes of Johannesburg to which it supplies cheap labour. Johannesburg is an all-white city. Blacks cannot swim in any of its 30 municipal pools. Black nurses cannot be treated or accommodated in the hospital where they tend the sick. And Johannesburg is run by the progressives.

Three years ago, nobody in Alexandra had heard of cricket. Then Bacher, seeing the futility of his current policies, consulted the powerful and prestigious ANC and built nets at a local school (motto: Reach for the Light). The game caught on. Helped by volunteer coaches the children practised all year round, and played matches against white schools. When the riots returned, the boys armed themselves with stones and protected their nets with all-night vigils. The school was damaged, but the nets remained untouched.

Now Alexandra has under-14 and under-15 teams. I went to see them play. Collecting the fellows at the nets, we found Peace and Justice batting. They are twins. In England twins are commonly called Alec and Eric. Little Harry was bowling. Harry has a stutter and didn't know what a hat-trick was until he took one last week. In a few days he was to fly to Port Elizabeth to represent Transvaal. Had he rung Dr Bacher yet for his ticket? If Bacher is being rung by 11-year-old black children, all is not lost.

Arrow, Solomon, Moses, Jack and Catphus had arrived. A blend of Zulus, Xhosa and Tsutu. Jack lives with 10 others in a two-room house, and once missed practice because it was his turn to wash under a tap shared by 50 people.

We drove merrily off in a mini-bus towards an all-white government school in a plush suburb, and found, upon arriving, boys in blazers and caps, waiting.

At first the games did not go well. Despite catching, running and concentrating with a skill surprising in those so new to the game, the boys were out-gunned. Then their delayed fast bowler turned up. It was like the relief of Mafeking. Chatter returned, battle rejoined.

After tea, the under-14s slipped to defeat, despite their magnificent catching. Meanwhile, Peace, Justice, Felix and Godfrey took their team to a victory whereupon, wonder of wonders, the boys lined up and shook hands. Then the players went their separate and shocking ways, to mansion and to shanty.

Apartheid is dying, the victim of demographic, economic and political pressures, a victim of time and numbers. The stick has done its stuff. I think cricketers should be allowed to go to coach in the townships, and the ICC should go to study their work. To fail to do so is mere cowardice.

They should also talk to the ANC about a graduated re-entry into Test cricket. They have to give some hope to the few people in South Africa who are trying to do something. Maybe it is time for a little of the carrot.

CRICKET'S LETHAL BOMB

Bump 'em down and keep 'em short,
It's the essence of the sport;
Bowl 'em very fast and short,
Make 'em bump, and that's the sort;
Hit him – body, head or wicket –
'Tis the soul of Modern Cricket,
And if he tries to score from you, he's certain to be caught.

For a few dreadful moments on Sunday it appeared as though Test cricket had suffered its first fatality. Geoff Lawson lay on his back, clutching his jaw. Fieldsmen waved frantically for a doctor, their concern evident.

Lawson's pain was clear. A stretcher was summoned and the patient taken away in an ambulance. Hours later Lawson was on the operating table.

Yesterday morning he said he was well, bore no grudges and wanted to play cricket at the weekend. Those first moments had been misleading. He was all right.

People should not forget their thoughts during those moments. A cricketer could have died. This fact must be faced in all its horror. Excuses can be made.

Lawson is a timid player of the quick stuff. Bowlers can smell his fear as a shark smells blood, and they attack it mercilessly. Foolishly, he was not wearing a grille on his helmet. Besides, this Perth is a bouncy pitch, cricket is a hard game and that's the way it goes. Clichés roll off the tongue with the smoothness of a Sinatra song.

But it will not do. Let us dispose of the misfortune which befell Lawson quickly, because it is not the real issue. Beyond argument we should not panic every time a cricketer is hurt. Whatever the rules, this will happen occasionally, particularly in Perth, where the bounce is unusually steep.

In any case, we do not want a game in which sissies can do as well as heroes. Nor is it good enough to blame the West Indians for the injury. If Australia or England had a quartet of fast bowlers they too would use them ruthlessly. And neither of them would be as sorely provoked by nasty remarks from drunks on the edge of the boundary as were these West Indians.

These are distractions. Forget, if you can, about Lawson's jaw. Recollect the bombardment of short-pitched balls dished out to Steve Waugh and Graeme Wood during the afternoon. Recollect the bumpers delivered by Merv Hughes earlier in the game, and conclude that far too many physically dangerous deliveries are being bowled in cricket. Not in every Test, but regularly enough to demand action. If a cure is not found the odds on somebody being killed will continue to rise.

It's no good expecting the umpires to deal with this threat. Authorities who point fingers at them are simply passing the buck. Is Terry Prue, veteran of 12 Shield games, expected to tell Isaac Vivian Alexander Richards that his team is infringing some vague rule?

Umpires do not want to brand themselves by being controversial. They know how little backing they might get. Accordingly, if weakly, they spend their time shaking their heads to leg before wicket shouts and enforcing the pettifogging no-ball rule which has so affected the first two Tests.

No realistic observer will blame either the players for playing to the rules or the umpires for failing in their ill-defined duties. It is up to the authorities to reduce the peril by passing carefully constructed rules limiting the number of lethal balls bowled. If they don't, they will carry a part of the guilt when someone is killed.

What can they do? They could allow only one, maybe two, balls to pitch in the bowler's half of the pitch in any single over. They could change the laws of field placing as they did after the bombardment of 1932–3, by allowing only three men to field behind point on the offside.

Fast bowling will continue to dominate Test cricket. Fast bowlers are getting taller, thinner, and their numbers are rising. Because the game is changing physically and athletically so the laws must change if violence is to be avoided.

It isn't much fun having a cricket ball directed at your head three times an over at 140km/h. You only have to get one wrong. For those standing at the hot end there must appear to be more to worry about than at any time since Bodyline. It is time to act.

Do not hold your breath. The poem quoted earlier was written in 1898. I fear for the Australians today.

A PERFUMED HARLOT

Why is it that we stuffed shirts find one-day games so irredeemably dull? After all, as poet Philip Hodgins has written of sport generally:

> It has a narrative that gets you in,
> A kind of play in which the final score
> Casts every move into its proper light;
> And whether it's rerun on giant screens
> That frown like Cyclops high above the grounds
> Or in the black and white consistencies
> Of Monday morning's double sporting spread
> The big effect will always be the same –
> Some disappointment that the moment passed
> Without a chance to see it as it was, not covered up with
>   television lights
> And ghastly logos from the corporate set.
> But naked human spirit on the line.

And there's the rub. One-day cricket is an unemotional game, as different from the real thing as soap opera is from tragedy. Spectators know it, of course, and they indulge in Mexican waves, cheer streakers and sing rude songs to show they are having a good night out and do not consider the cricket to be unduly serious.

These games seldom engage the human spirit and certainly never strip it naked because underneath the whipped up frenzy, apart from the screams and shouts and ignoring the hard sell of knowing commentators, it is matter of fact to the point of banality, a drunken orgy where once there beat a heart.

Banality finds its expression in the cheapening of tactics and skill. Field placements are predictable, though less so when Allan Border is captain, and great bowlers cut their pace and find themselves trundling without slips, serving up deliveries solely to prevent batsmen smiting, as if their hard-won skill meant nothing. Wasim Akram bowling to Dean Jones in a Test match is a magnetic duel, a battle of class and a study in technique in which neither man is compromised for both can dictate the course of events. Their duels in the one-day contests are without significance for both men are restricted by rules, like a writer in a totalitarian State.

Is this blunt enough? To adore one-day cricket is to choose a perfumed harlot. It is an escape, a neglect of what is important. With their ghastly logos, big screens and a 'hundred thousand rowdy fans who want something that's lacking in themselves' these games are hypnotic and cheap.

Quite simply one-day cricket fails to challenge the spirit because a player's choices are reduced. He cannot reach into himself to summon a stubborn innings lasting days to save his hide, cannot sustain an attack when he is in command, cannot match himself against a great opponent on his game.

Partnerships such as that constructed by Imran Khan and Akram in Adelaide are impossible, and distinguished players are like a grandmaster trying his hand at quick chess into which foolish errors creep and about which grandmasters usually laugh uproariously.

Nor will anything produced yesterday survive as long in the memory as Aravinda de Silva's 100 in Brisbane or Mark Greatbatch's sustained resistance in Perth, for this was the stuff of greatness.

One-day cricket offers a top night out with the boys (or girls), a cheerful and communal spirit and some cricket which can be exciting in its climaxes, so much so that they might as well play five 20-over chases at agreed targets or five 10-over contests on the same evening.

Test cricket, on the other hand, is a study of human nature in which men reveal themselves, sometimes sadly as Chris Matthews did last year in Brisbane.

I write, of course, as an unapologetic stuffed shirt, as someone who finds soul in Test cricket and a suspicious shallowness in these jovial exchanges. Let it be said that they have their moments; even yesterday Jones played one scintillating front foot square cut.

And let it be said that they guarantee periods of attacking cricket and 100-overs of play to boot, none of which is promised when a Test begins. Nevertheless, this cricket is a performance rather than an examination which is, perhaps, the way of modern sport.

IN PRAISE OF
SPORTSMANSHIP

In the none-too-distant past we have had all manner of unsavoury events on the field. We have seen aluminium bats, players kicking one another, men run out for backing up (in defiance of tradition and manners), and appeals made when a batsman is so ill-advised as to pick up the ball to return it to the bowler.

All this has been done in the name of the great god masculinity, as if these childish antics had anything to do with proper conduct. Sport has given us many gentle, impressive heroes; now a lie is being perpetrated that success on the field demands arrogance and vitriol. We do not hear about Bjorn Borg but about John McEnroe, not about Wes Hall but about Sarfraz on one of his less benevolent days.

Excuses have been made for conduct for which any schoolmaster worth his salt would have delivered a hefty kick in the offender's rear. In fact, some deeds were not merely excused, they were advocated. A player, it was said, must act like a spoiled brat or he was not really giving of his best.

Now it is being suggested that if only the Australian team was nastier it might win more often. Tim Zoehrer and Craig McDermott believed this poppycock and what have they achieved? Marsh, Waugh and Reid ignored it and they seem to be managing.

Allan Border has done cricket a great service. He does not spit or snarl, does not rail against umpires or shriek about bad luck. Border has blamed no-one but himself and his colleagues for their defeats this summer. He has not allowed his despair to affect his behaviour on the field. He has brought no indignity upon the game, and for this he deserves our thanks.

Not every man in the Australian and England teams is beyond reproach. In Melbourne and Perth spectators had to endure what in my opinion were the juvenile antics of McDermott and Zoehrer. Upon taking a wicket at the MCG, McDermott grimaced, punched the air, pointed to the pavilion and appeared to shout in the manner of a Sioux warrior at a war dance. He cannot be taken seriously as a cricketer until he conducts himself with the dignity shown by his colleagues in this and other sports.

Zoehrer, I believe, was foolish in Melbourne and petulant in Perth. In Melbourne he greeted the arrival of Phil Edmonds at the crease with comments Edmonds found offensive.

Happily, the crowd was warm and polite – as crowds have been throughout the tour. Gladstone Small took five wickets in the Australians' first innings and in a restaurant that night the diners rose to applaud him. Despite the hard times, scarcely a nasty remark has been heard from the stands.

None was heard at Kooyong, either, so it is not a matter of victory and defeat. This, surely, has been helped by the responsible attitudes of the cricketers and tennis players.

In any case, Zoehrer got his come-uppance, first when Edmonds, noticing that Zoehrer had dropped the ball not for the first time, turned to him and said: 'Still fumbling them, I see.' Secondly, Edmonds wandered into the Australian dressingroom next day to recite an ode which began

Australia has a keeper called Zoehrer
Whose work gets poorer and poorer . . .

Despite these sound tactics Zoehrer was silly again in Perth, exchanging words with Pakistan's Qasim Omar, whereupon he was rebuked by the Australian manager, Bob Simpson. It is to be hoped that this reprimand was not a gesture.

Australia has a reputation for hard and fair play. Its tennis players and golfers are respected for their fierce determination and for their friendliness. In cricket, the same tradition of fierce competition on the field and hospitality off it has applied. Throughout its history Australia has won lots of Test matches. Only in the past decade did the cursing mentality defile the game. Border has restored the good name of Australian cricket.

And is he now to be dropped as Australia's captain and replaced by Dirk Wellham? Was not Wellham the chap who so nearly turned aside from Australian cricket to join Kim Hughes in South Africa? Was he brought back to the fold by a sense of duty? And is he now to succeed the steadfast Border? Say it is not so.

ACADEMY TEACHES WHAT MOST LEARN FAR TOO LATE

AUSTRALIAN cricket's latent hostility to its Adelaide academy can be understood easily. Anything elitist provokes feeling here because it brings forth images of starched collars and pompous Poms. In Adelaide, a bloke is a bloke be he born n'er so high or n'er so low. He expects to be called mate and regards a fair go as his birthright. If people were separated like wheat from chaff on this baked and remote land, what on earth would be the point of it all? Might as well go and live in Sussex.

Moreover, Australians are suspicious of fads, proud of their firm grip on life which consigns mantras and muesli to their various dustbins. Cricket Academy has this ring to it, and sounds like a bandwagon on which the inadequate jump, a pretension dedicated to turning out moderately gifted cricketers, an introversion contemplating its own navel.

So forget about this phrase Cricket Academy, for really it isn't like that at all, as I will testify having spent a few days training with its 14 students.

Every morning begins at journalistic dawn (7.45 am) with a hard training session. Anyone arriving late is fined $1 a minute, money deducted from negligible wages, food and accommodation having been laid on. Monday is the toughest day, a time for renewing fitness and loosening joints. Fitness is important in cricket these days, says director David Sincock, a former State player, who is proud of the fielding and running of his charges. Probably it was unwise to pick Monday for a first sampling.

On mustering, an immediate impression arose of 14 lively youngsters carrying not an extra ounce of flesh and who had, nevertheless, a democratic sparkle in their eyes. A jolly crew, they teased each other about their results in grade cricket on Saturday and also mentioned various weekend activities which reminded this correspondent that this was an academy, not a monastery. They were a typical bunch of spirited youths bonded by a single purpose, to succeed in cricket. Camaraderie was strong because they had been working together since March.

And, my word, training was rigorous this particular Monday morning. We ran around parks and began an apparently endless series of sprints at which the *Herald* did not disgrace itself. After 45 minutes we returned to the Adelaide University gym and were put through a fierce routine of exercises which included burtees, called McDermotts by these lads who say Craig can do 188 in five minutes. Strugglers were urged on by their mates and soon their shirts were wringing wet. A second round was decided on and these enthusiasts scrapped their 30-second rest interval. As the heat rose and bones ached someone yelled 'keep going, lads, think of Thursday'. That was the day they were to meet England's premier cricketers.

Our session finished at 10 am. There is swimming, weight-lifting and skipping on other mornings. Students are free from 10 am to 3 pm and are supposed to find work, or study for a degree. Greg Bluett works in a bank, Simon Cottrell is a glazier, David Castle mows lawns and Lawrie Harper chops things up, sometimes including his own fingers. Daniel from Darwin studies, but others simply wander off to Glenelg Beach, which is not good enough, for going ga-ga is a constant threat here. At Glenelg they visit Jack Potter's kiosk; Potter started the academy with Peter Spence three years ago and resigned in October, apparently after failing to win appointment to manage Australia's youth team in the Caribbean – a team consisting entirely of his students.

Damien Martyn, acknowledged as the gun player, goes to the Adelaide Oval to practise with Justin Langer and Shane Warne, a leg spinner from Victoria who gives it a terrific flick. Barry Causby, former Croweater batsman is their technical coach. Old hands, like Jim Higgs, help occasionally. Coaching is not over-done, this is not an assembly line. Players are allowed to express themselves, provided they are striving for excellence. Damien bowls energetically, bats with challenge and wears an earring. Shane has blond cropped hair, an exuberant spirit and also occasionally dons an earring – what Bill Lawry will make of him cannot, at this distance, safely be predicted. Their chums are rather more orthodox, but I saw no hint of aggression being dimmed, while talks on matters psychological and nutritional were merely advisory.

At 3.30 pm on this Monday we returned for a tough and

boisterous bout of aerobics. Afternoons are usually reserved for carefully organised and vigorous practices, or for matches.

Can this idea work? As Chandrasekhar could testify, all sorts of people can succeed in cricket. Nevertheless, no sound reason exists to prevent a country, serious about cricket, from choosing 14 youngsters each year and giving them concentrated instruction without guaranteeing success. Already, 18 have played Shield cricket and students eagerly await a first Test cap. In March they will return to their studies or to the workforce having been taught what most of us learn far too late.

WHY THE CAPTAIN LAY DOWN AND CRIED

LAST week, dramatically, Australia's cricket captain resigned. His team was 2-0 down in the series, and was being outplayed by the magnificent West Indians. He had himself dropped several easy catches, and twice thrown away his wicket.

And yet he did not resign because of cricket, nor because he would have been sacked if he had not resigned. Australia have not yet lost the series, there is no obvious candidate of calibre to succeed and no-one can entirely blame a captain whose team is not good enough.

Kim Hughes was forced out. He succumbed to the cumulative venom of critics who rejoiced at his every impetuosity, who were determined to nail him. In the end, they succeeded. His was a hot-headed decision taken in haste, and delivered with tear-jerking emotion.

Hughes has plenty of enemies. His most savage critic was the sour, grizzly Ian Chappell, the man who led the World Series Cricket rebellion in 1977. He saw Hughes as a blue-eyed boy, a favoured son of the establishment and even in live interviews before Test matches, heaped scorn upon him.

Nor were Dennis Lillee and Rodney Marsh (who had played under Hughes) slow to condemn him. They too spat at Hughes's impetuosity; they too felt that he was the chosen man of the establishment who had risen to the top without serving an appropriate apprenticeship. They loathed his polish and laughed at his rashness.

This hostility to Hughes has its origins in the 1977 tour to England, the tour on which the Packer split was revealed. Of Greg Chappell's team, only Craig Serjeant and Hughes remained loyal to their governing board. Hughes's reward was mixed. He was selected for only one Test match in that series, being left out for Ritchie Robinson and Ian Davis; he condemned himself in the eyes of his peers as a tool of the establishment, but he won the captaincy of his country.

As Ian Chappell was dropping his trousers, as Lillee was throwing his aluminium bat, as Marsh was betting on England, Hughes was presenting himself as the knight in shining armour destined to rescue the honour of his country's cricket.

Hughes could have defeated his enemies had he been a successful or disciplined captain. As it is, he led his team to victory in only four out of 28 Tests, and still plunged into foolhardy adventures. He remains a professional cricketer unable to convince his colleagues of his leadership and maturity. To the contrary, he has loaded his enemies' guns.

Years ago, he charged Willis's bowling immediately after lunch in a Test match. His idea, apparently was to surprise the fast bowler, in fact, he surprised everyone on the ground by lifting the ball to mid-off. Last March, frustrated by the tactics of a weak Trinidad team, Hughes ordered his batsmen to defend when they were left with only an hour or so to bat. No-one wanted to bat with him, for his team-mates realised the silliness of this conduct. In the end, Greg Matthews accompanied his captain in his pointless protest. Everyone else was embarrassed.

This Australian season, Hughes has continued his erratic ways, mixing the poised excellence of his batting with strange rushes of blood. Twice he's been caught hooking. The second time, in Brisbane, he could not bring himself to follow the path of the ball into Marshall's hands. He stood, head bowed, like some schoolboy who had just broken a window, until the cheers of the West Indians informed him of his fate. With Ian Chappell perched in the commentator's box, with Greg Chappell and Rick McCosker (another 1977 tourist) selecting the team, he might as well have tightened his own noose.

And yet there had been signs that, at last, the hero was maturing. In the West Indies, a more stable captain emerged, or so it appeared. Relieved of the company of Lillee and Marsh (with friends like these . . .) and with Border subdued, Hughes forged a spirit resilient enough to save the first two Test matches, even though they lost the series 3-0. In India a few weeks ago, Australian morale soared when they easily won a one-day series, and Hughes must have felt the worst was over.

If he thought so, if he thought his enemies had changed their opinion or forgiven his 'treachery' of 1977, he was sadly mistaken. This season Ian Chappell and his followers have pounded away, and in the end Hughes resigned. Probably his resignation was another erratic decision, another of the infuriatingly hurried acts which have prevented Hughes leading Australia as well as his board of control had hoped.

Probably Hughes was a poor captain, and did not deserve to survive so long. But his resignation had little to do with his weaknesses. It was the result of a concerted campaign. The favoured son had finally been crushed.

GATTING

I⊤ was 3.30 on a Sunday afternoon in Melbourne just after
Christmas, a time for sport in Melbourne, as is every other time.
Down the road at Kooyong, Australia was beating Sweden in the
Davis Cup Final, a contest closely followed in the vast amphi-
theatre of the MCG. Yuletide spirit flowed freely in the bays as
Pat Cash fought back to beat Pernfors.

Things were not going so well for the locals in the cricket
stadium. Merv Hughes, of the toilet-brush moustache was the
last line of resistance, and his resistance is of the Maginot variety:
it is easily circumvented. He had just swept Edmonds to the
boundary. Gatting, his round Henry VIII face uncluttered by
frowns, moved Small a few yards to the left. Dutifully Hughes
blocked the next delivery, and the crowd, recognising heroic
restraint when it saw it, cheered. Then, his work done to his
satisfaction, Hughes swept and lifted a catch to the very spot
so recently occupied by Gladstone Small, who took the chance
gleefully. England had held the Ashes. Gatting's move had been
correct, as had so many of his previous moves, players grabbed
stumps and hugged each other. David Gower (who Gatting says
'isn't emotional when he scores 200') shook his friend's hand,
acknowledging his right to lead. And so began the celebrations
which were, apparently, to end up so colourfully a few hours
later in Elton John's hotel suite.

Throughout the southern summer England had played far
beyond prediction. Few had expected Gatting to return with the
Ashes, yet he did so easily and, for good measure, brought back
with him cups won in Perth, Sydney and Sharjah besides. It
wasn't only the weak Australians who had been beaten. (The
current joke in cricket was that Allan Border would retire from
first class cricket but continue as Australian captain.) Victories
were recorded against the West Indies and Pakistan too, so that
Gatting returned home as the most triumphant, though not the
most fêted, England captain since Sir Len Hutton (1954–55),

maybe since Douglas Jardine (1932–33). Under his leadership an extraordinary metamorphosis had occurred. A team thrashed in the West Indies, beaten by India and New Zealand, had forced its way back near to the top of the tree.

Gatting had said he wanted to restore English cricket to its rightful position, and, to widespread surprise, he'd done so. It was an astonishing turnabout, not least because the man in charge appeared to be ordinary to the point of dullness.

Mike Gatting's most documented characteristic is his penchant for putting Branston pickle in his sandwiches. Woe betide the 12th man who forgets to include a bottle of pickle on the tea trolley. He also apparently favours plates of salad piled high with chips. One youngster on the Middlesex staff says he eats 'a vast amount'. Tucking into pickles and chips isn't supposed to be a cricket captain's preponderant personality trait. It is difficult to portray such a man as enigmatic, let alone mystical. Brearley had been incredibly wise. Willis had been fast and mysterious (if only because he never said much). Botham had been wonderfully outrageous, satisfactorily exotic, and plainly doomed. Gower had quaffed champagne and passed wry comments. All were good copy. But what could be made of dear old 'Fat Gatt'? He appeared to be a confoundedly ordinary man. Fantasy plays no part in his character. What you see is what you get. He is as round as a beer-barrel, has a voice that pipes, and does not pretend to style. He gives the impression of being a plodder, particularly to those who study his words rather than his deeds. He recognises this, says that his image will not change now and that he 'wants the ball to go to the boundary. I'll do it my way. If they ordain this to be graceful that is fine. Usually they say I clobbered it. Crikey, it's gone, that's the main thing.'

Yet it was this Gatting who was in charge during England's remarkable winter abroad. He deserves to be congratulated for his leadership.

Even his origins are prosaic. His parents raised him in Collingwood and he attended Wickham primary school where a Mrs Collister organised 20-over games, in one of which Gatting scored a hundred. He graduated to a local comprehensive school, John Kelly's Boys High ('the girls were next door') and can boast of being the first England captain to be schooled in a comprehensive (Botham attended a secondary modern). Gatting didn't play much cricket at John Kelly's, concentrating upon soccer in which game he once had a trial at Watford. It is easy to picture him as a battling ball-winner in midfield. Probably he was a gifted forward.

His cricket career resumed when he answered an advertisement, placed in the Willesden and Brent Chronicle, from Brondesbury CC. His route to the top thereafter was orthodox, almost routine. He rose through the ranks at Brondesbury, with Middlesex schools, and finally with E.S.C.A. At every level his pugnacity was recognised and rewarded. Gatting did not demur from the view of himself as the outstanding hope of London cricket. We are all outstanding on the way up, living in a fool's paradise, forgetting that in other areas other talents are maturing.

It is, so far, an unspectacular tale. No obstacle had been encountered. Gatting's character was a mixture of naivety and bumptiousness. He says he was always giving the other person the benefit of the doubt, as if casting his mind back to an earlier time, before the gathering of scepticism. He batted as he talked, with a cockiness which was later to irritate his seniors, though Gatting was scarcely aware of this at the time.

He was a precocious youth, this star of Wickham, John Kelly's, Brondesbury and Middlesex. It appeared inevitable that he'd soon be sitting at the head of English cricket. This did not happen, and for a decade his career waxed and waned to such a degree that failure was confidently predicted and a loss of nerve diagnosed. His decline began in 1977 and lasted until 1984. It was not much of a decline really, not in the eyes of most cricketers. Gatting scored lots of county runs and played in lots of Test matches. But he did not establish himself in the England team, and did not fulfil his prodigious talent for batting. Slowly he felt himself to be drifting away from the core of the team. He felt like an outsider and he batted like one. His experiences in those years in which others hogged the limelight imbued in Gatting the steel absent in his background. He matured into a man with the quiet anger of the dispossessed. These years of surprising, perhaps unjust, struggle eventually gave to England a captain of calibre, one who did not belong to the old gang.

Sipping a glass of wine in the garden of the Enfield home in which he lives with his wife ('we've known each other a long time . . . about twelve years isn't it? . . . is that right, darling?'), his two young sons and his mother-in-law (it's her house), Gatting recalled his first, vital, tour to Pakistan and New Zealand in

1977–78, a tour which had a marked effect on his career. He'd considered himself lucky to be chosen (Gower was not picked) and felt rather bogus in the illustrious company.

Suddenly the cocky kid was mixing with Boycott and Willis, greats of the game. He played in a Test match in Karachi but otherwise did not distinguish himself. For the first time he felt ill at ease, surplus to requirements. Throughout his career, whenever Gatting has felt this way he has failed. He is a bubbly man and the natural instinct of elders is to prick the bubble. Deflated, Gatting was nervous and tentative. In Karachi he twice lost his wicket to lbw decisions. He'd shove his front foot down the pitch, forsaking his free approach, like a Derby winner forced to gallop for his oats. His habit when he is too tense is to move his foot early and across the stumps, a movement which cramps the swing of the bat. Gatting's Test career is frustratingly littered with lbw decisions caused by this fault.

It did not help, either, that after Brearley's arm was broken, Geoffrey Boycott took over as captain. Boycott imposed his own dedication on his team, demanding that they bat correctly and practise diligently. Perhaps this added to Gatting's inhibitions. For him a less introverted approach is appropriate. But Gatting's failures in New Zealand cannot be blamed entirely upon his betters. Boycott's approach did not suit one wild youth from Yeovil, either. Far from being nonplussed by the old maestro, Botham teased him and, when the opportunity arose, ran him out. He, at least, was having none of Boycott's solemnity.

As if the first taste of failure was not enough to depress Gatting, he suddenly found a rival in this hulk from Somerset. On this tour began the rivalry between Botham and Gatting that has percolated ever since. Botham had been chosen as the second white hope of the tour. These two beefy combatants fought first for the spotlight (Botham was taken even less seriously than Gatting – Brearley wondered why he'd been brought) and later for supremacy. In a state game before the first Test match in New Zealand it was obvious that there was one place, and one place only, to be won by Gatting or Botham. Gatting failed twice. Botham recorded a duck in the first innings, missed his pair by 'a gnat's whisker' in the second, and finished with a century, described in Wisden as 'brilliant'. Botham played in all three Test matches, performing heroics. Gatting was chosen only for the last Test in Auckland where he failed to trouble the scorers in his only innings. These were considerable blows to his esteem.

Brearley believes that there was, from the start, 'quite a bit of feeling' between the two men, and that Gatting felt a sense of 'inferiority and injured pride'. For the next five years, before the troubles began, Botham swept magnificently across English cricket while Gatting battled to prove himself. It would have been an easier ride if he'd meekly accepted his role as second fiddle. Gatting's competitive instincts tolerated no such timidity. He did not humbly fade into the background, living in the wake of a mightier force. As a result for the next six years he defied his gift with a string of bewildering setbacks. He had his moments – scoring well under Brearley in the great if ultimately misleading 1981 series – but he was passed by Botham, Gooch, Gower and Lamb. Instead of being the main man he found himself shoved up and down the order at the whim of a captain. Worse, he quickly realised that his failure to play the part of doting follower was costing him dear. Neither Willis nor Botham held him in high regard, and he did not belong to their crowd. Still sipping his wine, and rising for once to animation, he remembered his time as one of the frowned-upon:

> I felt I wasn't wanted. I was there because they had to pick me. This lasted until David (Gower) took over. You can tell when someone believes in you and you can tell when someone thinks you've had enough chances. I overheard one bloke say to a captain that now I was in the team I might get eight Test hundreds. The captain replied that I'd better hurry up because I wouldn't be in the team long. This man was commentating when I scored my seventh Test hundred in Australia.

Used to running the show, used to being the man in charge, Gatting did not adapt well to his bit part. He did not enjoy being cast as the perpetual pretender, was not prepared to lower his sights. He is a man who wants to be in the thick of things, he wants to compete and to belong. His chirpy cockney pride demands it. This period on trial did not suit him, yet frustratingly he could not break out. As Ian Botham remarked, Gatting batted differently in Test matches; he changed his game. He was cautious and inhibited. In county cricket he'd belt the ball; in Test matches he tried to build an innings.

His wobbliest moment – his nadir (not the Pakistan spinner) – came against the West Indies in 1984. Three times he lost his wicket without so much as offering a stroke. One youngster on the Middlesex staff advised him to put his bat-stickers on upside-down in order not to cheat his sponsors, so often was he pictured on the back pages, bat held aloft and umpire's finger raised. (This intrepid youth is now enjoying his cricket on the South Coast.) Critics began to write of Gatting as one of those men who, for obscure reasons, freeze in the Test match arena. By the end of the 1984 season he was a spent force, or so it appeared. He went back to Middlesex determined at least to lead his side well and to score lots of county runs.

Then he was chosen, out of the blue it seemed, for the winter's tour to India. He was picked at the insistence of David Gower, the least starstruck of the top cricketers, and the most independent. Moreover Gower chose Gatting as his vice-captain, an inspired move which restored to his friend all the audacity on which he relies. To add to this sudden shaft of light, Botham had already decided to spend a winter at home, preparing for his benefit. These fortunate changes gave Gatting an importance lacking so far in his Test career. Gower also demanded the inclusion of the irascible Edmonds. Everyone could see that the old guard was finished.

Gower's tour to India was happy and victorious, and is still spoken of by players as the most enjoyable trip of all. On it Gatting proved himself at last as a convincing batsman in international cricket, scoring a double century and another hundred.

He did enough to silence his harshest critic. He was the master now, not the unwanted servant.

This winter's tour was the turning point in Gatting's career. Things have not been entirely plain sailing since – in 1985 his nose was spread across his face by a Marshall bouncer, and his brave return was halted at once by a broken thumb – but he was in command, if not in charge. Nor had he lost his bumptiousness, except that it had begun to look like courage. He had never backed down from Botham, had never given second best as a man, and in Barbados he showed his mettle. Reacting to a pointed comment by Gatting ('I was frustrated with my injury, and with the way he was batting. He kept blaming the pitches'), Botham barked that he was not to be spoken to as a child. Gatting made it clear that he'd speak to him like a child while ever he batted like one. Their relationship had returned to an equilibrium lost on that first tour. And it continued just so. Botham was not in the team when Gatting was appointed to replace Gower as captain. Gatting made it plain to Botham upon his return after serving a suspension that he expected him to toe the line, at practice and on the field, an approach advocated by Brearley. In Australia last winter he insisted that every player use the nets properly. Moreover Gatting used Botham well as a bowler, unleashing him when the force was with him and leaving him in the slips when it wasn't. It helped, of course, that this was Botham's last tour, that he intended to play domestic cricket in Australia in the following winter, and that he was keen to stay out of trouble. Nevertheless the great allrounder has not, in his pomp, been better handled by any captain than he was by Gatting.

In fact Gatting's captaincy throughout the winter was distinguished, at times even inspired (as when he decided to field first in Melbourne – a decision described by Richie Benaud as extraordinary). His approach was not particularly subtle. He simply left his best players to get on with it, having first set the tactical pattern in conference with Micky Stewart and the senior cricketers. At times he disappeared to the boundary, partly because several of his men could not throw, and partly to show his faith in his team. He used his fast bowlers as a strike force, and his Middlesex spinners as stock bowlers, controlling the game while Dilley and the others rested. His field placing was shrewd, though at times cautious and unimaginative (largely because England had not won a Test series for some time).

Most significant of all, he lifted the team when all appeared lost before the first Test match. England had not played well in the run up to the Brisbane Test, so Gatting called a meeting which he later described as 'tremendous'. He believed that the problem was that several of his players had toured so often before that they were bored with practice games. He found them eager for the battle for the Ashes. He chose his best team irrespective of previous form, though caution dictated the inclusion of Jack Richards to bolster the batting. Finally, and with typical lack of profundity, Gatting decided to ease the pressure on the ailing Gower by taking upon himself the responsibility of batting at first wicket down. Actually it wasn't quite like that:

> We hadn't decided who should go in three. Lamb and Stewart wanted me to. Then a few minutes before the toss I asked David – who was in the gents at the time – where he was going to bat. He

said he didn't mind. I said "It's O.K. if I go in 3?" He said "fine",
so I strapped on the pads and off we went.

No less typically, Gatting's team-talk went along the lines of
'We've just got to go out there, play straight and get stuck in',
none of which prevented him playing an irreligious hoick before
settling down to reach fifty. Gower also returned to form with a
half-century.

Though he batted well on this tour – hitting a hundred in Adelaide and scoring well in Perth and Sydney – Gatting probably is
yet to fulfil himself as a Test match batsman. Brearley thinks he
could be more classical and finds his game to be faintly disappointing, particularly in his failure to correct the flaws exposed
by the greatest of modern bowlers, Richard Hadlee. Brearley
believes that Gatting still has more to offer as a player. Nevertheless he was a considerable force throughout the 1985–86 series.

England won the series handsomely, though the 2-1 margin
did not express their superiority. Gatting did lead his team with
distinction. To the task of captaining England he brought a
remembrance of those years of struggle. He did not forget the
rejections, and under his stewardship England's cricket was
open, healthy and without rancour (though Gatting did show his
bloody-minded streak in failing to recall a Pakistani batsman
who walked in Perth in the mistaken belief that he was out). Yet,
somehow, Gatting still appeared at times to be curiously at odds
with his surroundings. He is, in so many ways, a man of ordinary
tastes, a man for pickle, chips and lager. Despite his position he
can still be hesitant, and perhaps this is why the quality of his
captaincy has not been recognised without reservation. At press
conferences he can be outstandingly obtuse, rolling out clichés
as if they were revelations. He addresses not the brightest and
soundest of the reporters, but the dimmest and most unworthy.
In Brisbane on the eve of the Test match he sat reading a copy
of *The Cricketer* as the journalists fired their questions at him. To
some this appeared to be contemptuous; others saw it as the
reaction of a man who did not feel in his element. Gatting's
explanation, as usual, was determinedly simple. He'd 'had to
fight for it upstairs in the team room. It'd just arrived through
the post and I was quite keen to keep my mitts on it'. Complexity
does not furrow his brow if he can help it.

He denies using clichés, disarmingly arguing that reporters

always ask the same questions to which he invariably gives the same answers. It is time, he believes, that turns them into clichés. This is nonsense. He can be stupendously cautious in his replies, an approach that aggravates his audience and causes him to be underestimated. 'Such an obvious chap,' the whisper goes around. Had not Brearley taken the art of captaincy toward fresh subtleties? There on a fatal shore, Gatting was bringing it back again. Brearley and Benaud, of course, were far more astute. Not only were they superb captains, they also had the knack of picking critical moments in games and pointing out how cunning their tactics had been at those times! Brearley believes that Gatting is so diffident because he finds it difficult to put himself across in an interesting way. Of course it is not essential for a captain to be interesting, not even in Press conferences. Gatting is not taken so seriously, particularly when the loquacious and helpful Micky Stewart is around to explain everything. How could so ordinary a man be taken seriously as a captain? But he is not ordinary, rather he is straightforward, wanting in the glib and oily art, a Cordelia of a man. He lacks charisma and charm, and is bluff and gruff.

And so Gatting isn't portrayed as the sagacious leader who has taken English cricket by the scruff of the neck, or as the man who has turned it around even more dramatically than did Brearley in 1981. This may hurt Gatting more than he cares to admit. He says he lacks 'Brearley's education' and says it doesn't worry him what people say so long as he gets the results. He talks a lot about getting results. He talks a lot, too, about his image and his education, more than might be expected in a man who is supposed not to care about either. He may be unfortunate that he is a leader who does not look as a leader is supposed to look, a splendid batsman who does not look as splendid batsmen are supposed to look, and a star who does not conduct himself as stars are supposed to do. What is left is a man who has played his part in restoring England's cricket to its previous good name, and to its previous high standing. He had been lucky in one respect, not yet having led England in a Test series against the West Indies (poor Botham, poor Gower). Nevertheless he has done marvellously well. He says 'respect has got to be earned. I had to earn the respect of the senior players. Perhaps I still do. But I hope I'm half-way there.' Rather further than that, some would say.

ON RETIREMENT

R<small>EFLECTING</small> upon his tranquil dotage, Quentin Crisp once said: 'I had come to the end of my personality, had done everything I was going to do.' Tomorrow will, in all probability, be the last of my 1,203 days as a Somerset cricketer. This innings, if it occurs, will be my 757th for the club.

Leaving will, of course, be an emotional wrench, for I am leaving not merely a club and its splendid supporters but a way of life so consuming that it occupies players all day every day for six months. In cricket there is no gradual decline through the divisions, rather a vast chasm awaiting those who leave its stage. No wonder so many ex-cricketers cannot manage. No wonder this one decided to depart when people were asking 'Why?' rather than 'Good God; are you still playing?'

Choosing a time to go was difficult. Money was a factor. Somerset hasn't got any. Three years of overspending saw to that (costs rose £200,000 from 1988 to 1989). Disturbing reports were spreading of local youngsters who cost hardly anything being blamed for this deficit and for first-team failures, while those truly accountable lay low.

Had not Jack Birkenshaw left, had not three senior players, myself included, chosen to go, hardly a youngster could have survived, because all of the many expensive players were on long contracts. How Somerset manoeuvred itself into this position is not for a humble servant to guess.

Nor did I want to deny such youngsters an opportunity I had hugely enjoyed, knowing as I did what shattered dreams being sacked involved. Accordingly, in June I told Somerset of my impending retirement, provided Chris Tavaré carried on playing. We wanted fresh blood. After all, we were bottom and broke.

Money was not the only factor. Cricket is a wonderful game but current county cricket is very disappointing. Uncontested runs and slow pitches are not to my taste. So many games involve two days of dull run-collecting, followed by batsmen blocking in anticipation of lob bowling, and ending with the artificial ecstasy of a run chase.

Having been raised to see cricket as a game of cut and thrust, I wanted no part of this cheapening of runs. Either I was right or Richard Harden is far and away the best player Somerset has ever produced, and Jimmy Cook the best player since Bradman. Both are superb players and both know this is wrong.

These events dulled my spirit and whenever I looked at the clock it said not 3.45 but 11.25. Perhaps I was getting too old for it all, and would soon be wearing my trousers rolled.

Nor was moving from being a general to a foot soldier a simple matter. As captain and as Vic Marks's senior adviser, I had been closely involved in a club dear to my heart. Suddenly outsiders were in charge, and I was a peripheral character, batting, bowling occasionally and fielding at long-leg from April to September.

My mind was too energetic for such anonymity, and plainly was in search of a role, especially as my own career was fading. Helping the local youngsters, regularly offering to stand down in their favour and bowling on big occasions back in the thick of things, sustained interest for a time, but gradually departure appeared the only resolution.

After all, who really cared if I scored more hundreds than Lionel Palairet or not? Critics may guess that Chris Tavaré and I were at daggers drawn, but nothing is further from the truth. Tavaré's qualities of patience, decency and faithfulness, perhaps to a fault, are obvious to all, and he has been a thoughtful captain. We drifted apart because we marched to the beat of different drums, that is all.

Upon arriving at a ground, he slowly removes his socks, neatly folds them and carefully places them in their allotted spot; whereas it is widely regarded as a bonus if I turn up wearing socks of the same colour. To succeed, he needed to turn cricket into a job, to discipline his mind, and routine and consistency of play and conduct were his gods.

To succeed, I needed to play with my heart, and was throughout unduly sensitive to atmosphere. Lacklustre cricket drove me to distraction and my mood was changeable. In short, Chris and I were friendly yet possessed of different principles and attitudes, a point plainly enough made. And both of us needed to lead to sustain our enthusiasm. Neither wanted to grapple for power, and once Tavaré was happy to continue, I withdrew gracefully.

If this all sounds downbeat I have done cricket and Somerset a disservice. We all criticise things we care about. Playing for Somerset has been overwhelmingly a pleasure and a privilege, even if at various times matters arising have proven exasperating, preventing fondly held hopes of building a team and a club full of pride and passion as its members deserve.

It has mostly been great fun, and even now amusing things occur. Once Roland Lefebvre, who is much given to waving his arms, lectured me at length about a cricketer's diet. We went for dinner. Much impressed, I ordered a Waldorf salad. He ordered a cheeseburger with everything.

Richard Bartlett was reading the final page of a detective story which he promised to give to me as soon as he finished. A minute later he shouted: 'Christ, she did it!' As for Cook, I did enjoy his one comment upon my batting this season: 'Hell, Roeby, if I was captain against you I'd definitely have a third man.

So I leave Somerset and presumably cricket with mixed emotions. Somerset must play with heart and spirit or perish, and a flavouring of young local talent is more vital than cavalier outsiders seem to understand. And talent can be found, not least in the excellent Caddick, Harden, Trump, Van Troost, Hallett and company.

Changes are vital in many areas if long-term success is sought, but now is not the time to enter such debates. Now is the time to wish everyone well, especially those who care most, and to thank colleagues for tolerating my lesser moments. I hope the brighter ones make it worthwhile.

To say I was exasperated by events off the field since 1988 would be to put it very mildly indeed. I have fought and fought and plainly the struggle naught availeth.

SUPERSTARS

RICHARDS

To see Isaac Vivian Alexander Richards take to the field in Jamaica, and elsewhere, is to hear a steady beat of drums and to picture an African potentate, all chains, furs and infernal eye, swaggering to his throne. For his is a grand entrance, one of poise, one which says 'see how far the little black boy from a tiny island has risen, see he cannot be blown away'.

Pride was beaten into Richards as a boy by his father, whom he reveres. And Richards has never forgotten to take pride in himself. He dresses magnificently, takes care of his body, is built like an egg-timer, and moves with regal disdain. He takes pride in his origins, too, and named his children Matara and Mali, African names which I found for him in history books.

This posturing conveys strength and certainty, and in private, too, he can sustain those he values. Eldine Baptiste, a fellow Antiguan and a sometime Test cricketer, once knocked on Richards's hotel door and, close to tears, explained his depression.

Richards told him: 'Remember your name, and take pride in it.' An hour later, Baptiste emerged ready to do battle and to take such blows as fell his way. This is Richards at his best, a godfather who demands fidelity and can instil strength.

He turned 39 this week, even as he overturned Sir Garfield Sobers's West Indies run record, and has been a titan of the game since he arrived, blazing away with the bat, in the early 1970s.

Criticisms are dismissed as if they were flea bites upon an elephant's hide because they are the words of parasites, people who know nothing of life on the front line. Yet he hears criticisms, hears rumours of disloyalty among his men and is angered by them for he is vulnerable to doubts about his leadership.

In these times, he can be vengeful, for though he is a religious man it is a religion of high church, of ritual, of chastisement, for vengeance is mine, saith the Lord. Anyone who is not a little afraid of this man, who walks into his auditorium with such style, does not know him. He is an open vein of emotion presenting himself as a grave elder.

To see Viv Richards batting is to witness this same struggle between righteousness and anger, and evermore the darker emotion is holding sway. As he grinds his chewing gum and sweats, mopping his brow with wristbands defiantly emblazoned in the colours of the rastafari (which is all Haile Selassie, dreadlocks, ganja and African roots), his head is still as a rock, hiding troubles, for to betray them is to be weak and Richards will never be weak.

But his batting tells its tale, with mellow periods of correct play, as in Adelaide two summers ago when he took a long net practice before batting and promptly constructed a careful innings, interspersed with scorching, violent upheavals during which Richards appears bent either on destroying the bowlers or himself.

His extraordinary Test hundred in 69 balls against England in Antigua seven years ago was one such violent outpouring, one such cyclonic devastation. And in this mood Richards pulsates, jigs and gathers himself in brutal assault. In this mood he is a cricketer of murderous intent, for Richards is no assassin, rather a hot-blooded player whose best innings have been played when his violence has been controlled and directed as it was during his greatest years, from 1976 to 1982, glorious years he has never quite recaptured. In those times he was a happier, easier man, and it showed.

These days, bat in hand, Richards hovers on the brink of eruption for he has a fury within which he cannot entirely control, no matter how hard he tries (and sometimes he tries hard).

In the 1970s, he burst upon cricket as a batsman of unparalleled joy and dazzling skill, a player who could rise to an occasion as he did when rebutting Tony Greig's notorious 'we'll make 'em grovel' jibe with innings awesome in their power and sustained authority.

No tall, white, imperious South African was going to put him down, and his innings included scores of 232 and 291 so that talk arose of a black Bradman, though Richards was never sufficiently in command of himself to follow so constant a course.

After all, he had been goaded by Greig, his blood aroused and his honour challenged. In this period of lightness, he also batted masterfully in Cup finals for West Indies and Somerset, seizing the greatest stages as champions do.

Only later did fallibility appear and, when it did, Richards was shaken, failing to win Cup finals for Somerset in 1982 and for the West Indies in 1983. In his first five years in Test cricket, Richards averaged 58.9. In his next five years 47.6 and in his last five years 45.6. Yet he has never had to face his own bowlers. His decline is documented.

In recent years, his game has embraced contempt for his fate, an uncompromising commitment to domination, a foaming fury because to him, cricket is a game of kill or be killed. It is a street fight in which it is up to umpires to keep the peace. He protects his territory.

As he aged he liked his world less, lost his innocence, and his temper boiled more easily so that his batting grew more reckless, though it could still be captivating. Most batsmen grow more canny as they age, as their blood cools; not Richards, for in him, and so in his batting, love and loathing do daily battle and when loathing is victorious his mind slips from control.

To see Viv Richards bowling is to see a warrior at play, for here is a cricketer of the jungle finding himself called on to roll over his arm, for even the mightiest players occasionally must serve.

Richards carries out this task with an amused, haughty air though woe betide a batsman who takes undue liberty; Richards does not care to be too heavily punished, has been around a long time, knows a few tricks. Sometimes, he even bowls in Test matches with the air of a man who regards spin as scarcely serious, a milksop's escape forced upon him by hosts who pre-pared pitches calculated to stifle his fast men.

Sensing a plot, believing he is being robbed, Richards can be stubborn, as he often is in Sydney, as he was in New Zealand once when he bowled 40 overs and never did take a second new ball because to do so was to be humiliated. Such tactics can surprise a team less inclined to see cricket as a battle for supremacy between races.

All of this is known, all of it acknowledged, and in our twilight years, we will remember his majestic batting and even his crafty bowling, remember it all as the work of a man reacting to his times.

And yet, so far as Richards's cricket goes, the best is yet to come, for it is his fielding which most captures the imagination. He appears to be dozing but he's peeping out of the corner of his eye in case a yard is pinched. (So it is in life – in Taunton, he slept with a bat by his bed in case of burglars.) On the field, sauntering around like a panther, a preened predator with an air of indolence and a beguiling tranquillity, he suddenly scents blood and, aroused, pounces in a blur of colour and athleticism as he did three times in the 1975 World Cup final, as he has done countless times since, shattering stumps with an Exocet throw or seizing upon an edge. At Lord's, he once stood on the boundary, ball at his feet, and teased Mike Gatting, inviting him to try for a second. Gatting, an intrepid character, strode three metres forward, was sent back by an appalled partner and did not make it.

Sometimes, this confidence strays too far and once Richards tried to catch a skier behind his back, a trick he had performed in a friendly. Alas, he dropped it this time and the words of Brian Close, his county captain, cannot, I fear, be printed in a family newspaper. Usually his fielding is brilliant.

This is a marvellous cricketer, a modern cricketer, fit, powerful and an advocate of competition rather than craft. He is a cricketer with a record practically without parallel, especially in limited-overs games, but he is a frustrated man, too, one for whom the sands of time are running out, for he is going bald, and his eyes have lost their rare sparkle, besides which he has endured several operations for haemorrhoids, a circumstance damaging to his pride and threatening to his health. This is a cricketer who feels himself incomplete.

Despite his wondrous if flawed batting, his other skills and his position as captain of the present Test champions – a title he has not lost during his years in charge – Richards is ill at ease. Tension can be detected in his laugh, high pitched, nearly a shriek, brittle and penetrating, not a loving laugh.

In good times, and there have been many, he laughs a lot for he can be amused and is amusing (unlike Ian Botham about whom few anecdotes are told). But it is not a laugh summoned from his belly, from the depths of his personality, for it has never been so easy.

Fires still burn within Richards, even stronger, if anything. On bad days, such as when he confronted an English journalist as his team was taking the field, he persuades himself the world is against him, though perhaps the reverse is truer; he broods upon this, reacts to it, believes he is being denied his just deserts.

After bursts of anger, sometimes frightening in their intensity, he never apologises yet does feel guilty and in the evening after he had argued with Geoff Lawson and Steve Rixon on the field in Sydney (differences had arisen about a decision), he met a stranger in a hotel lift and answered his questions at length, going so far as to hold the lift doors open until he had finished.

He can be portrayed as a despot, sometimes acts like one, yet wants to be believed and understood, for often he is in the right though his public relations, though his timing and manner can be wrong. No-one needs reach far into Richards to find the cause of this growing mistrust of his world. His father, a stern, fervent prison warder, taught him to fight for his rights, his island was a neglected backwater and his people were persecuted. He has forgotten none of this.

In 1973, when we first met, he seemed shy and a cricketer strong off the back foot, for his exotic front-foot drives through mid-wicket were a product of English pitches. His brilliance was obvious to those who saw the bedlam his batting created rather than the means he used – older pros thought he hit too often across the line, a criticism also directed at Bradman who did not do so badly either. He adopted humble friends, just one or two, distanced himself from the collar-and-tie brigade and trained hard, running around the ground to the amusement of some. They aren't laughing now.

His tension was less immediately obvious and I did not detect it until 1974 when we shared a hotel room in Northampton: he as an emerging star, I as a callow youth attending to 12th man duties. Every morning, he exercised vigorously in our room and one evening we went out for dinner.

After a time an argument began about black power, Roebuck saying it was as bad as white power, Richards saying the black man's time had come. So loud did debate rage that other guests stopped to study its source.

For rage it was, though for years it was hidden behind politeness and the sheer spontaneity of his cricket. Then, around 1982, life betrayed Richards, private misfortune striking hard and costing him dear which he has acknowledged but is left alone. He has never been quite so easy in his heart or in his cricket since, for he is an unforgiving man and grew suspicious of a world which had betrayed him.

Bitterness is a crippling emotion, and one inappropriate in a leader. Nowadays, his batting is a celebration of violence as much as of quickness of eye, deadliness of stroke and abandon of movement. Moreover, his unease keeps even friends at a distance, for you do not build a house at the base of a volcano.

Had he proved himself as a great captain he could have endured his gradual decline more easily, a decline caused in part by the ferocious demands made of Test cricketers these days. He had nourished hopes of emerging as a statesman, as a Clive Lloyd, dropped himself down the order and fielded at slip to bring seriousness to his image. But his blood is too hot, his combative streak too deep and the crown has lain uneasily upon his head.

In Adelaide two years ago, he launched a tirade at umpire Tony Crafter, so ferocious Crafter said he had never heard anything like it and never wanted to again (not that Channel 9 noticed anything untoward). Richards was reprimanded by his board and may even have repented. Yet inside, his fury was unabated.

And so he is still, utterly determined to go with a bang not a whimper, a fierce competitor, a boxer really rather than a cricketer, a man who finds it difficult to tolerate inadequacy, a man at odds with a game founded upon English traditions. Perhaps he ought to have been a boxer, for he can fight; he contemplated this sport but, laughing, admits he rejected it because his looks might be disturbed.

He has left cricket with much to remember, for he has been a majestic, charismatic, fit and explosive cricketer. Yet, frustration endures because he has not quite risen to his full stature as a man, has battled too often with the present to see clearly a route up the mountains he had once hoped to climb.

BOTHAM IN 1985

B<small>Y</small> Wednesday evening Ian Botham had scored 473 runs off the 345 deliveries bowled to him in first class matches this season: 362 of these runs had been struck either to or over the boundary. At the crease he has been a storm, a violent, rolling thunder which changes the atmosphere at his every appearance. His runs have been scored, not with the flashing hits of a Jessop but with the authority of a Hammond.

Botham's batting has not merely been powerful; it has been skilful too. This spring he has played his shots better than at any time in his career, especially the on-drive which he had never previously mastered. Botham is a superb back player – pulling, driving and hooking – and has a fierce off drive. But his legside strokes have tended to angle square of the wicket. This season they have been thumping through mid-on.

Cricketers are a sceptical lot. Fellows have slept under snooker tables when the mighty Richards is in full cry (or did they suppose I was still in?). Brilliance can appear commonplace when you see it every day. Somerset players have been astounded by the sustained majesty of Ian Botham's batting this May and have watched every ball. He has scorned timidity, blasting away with awesome power. His *tour de force* was delivered on Wednesday at Taunton.

Malcolm Marshall and Tim Tremlett had reduced Somerset to 108 for six. Marshall had, I thought, been bowling rather fast. Fast enough, at any rate, to break my finger.

The pitch at Taunton was moist and the morning damp, as white porridgy clouds hid the sun. Somerset's limping innings was rescued by Botham's masterpiece. Within an hour he had forced Marshall, still tearing in, to defend the boundary with five men. Marshall tried a yorker; Botham's bat, which is like a railway sleeper, dropped on it, and sent the ball scuttling past umpire Sam Cook, who says he's never seen a finer innings, and he's a cussed old beggar, is Sam.

Marshall fired down a bumper which reared at Botham's chin. The batsman swivelled, ducking his head under the danger and cracked the ball over square leg. Every verb must be violent. Marshall peppered Botham with fast balls pitched short of a length, jumping into his stomach. A hasty back defence for the rest of us, but Botham pulled them to mid-wicket, blows of raw courage, hits disdaining the whisper of 'take care, take care.' I don't think anyone else can clobber cricket balls travelling at 85 mph through mid-wicket with a crossed bat. You don't sleep under snooker tables when that sort of thing is going on.

Twice he missed his strike; a drive eluded point, and an edged hook struck a spectator on the head. Apart from these misjudgements every hit was an execution, every moment a decision.

Lesser bowlers suffered too. Tremlett, a worthy line and length man who was settling in to his rhythm, was smashed to the old pavilion. He had taken three wickets in a few overs in his nagging, awkward way, but this blow put an end to that. This is Botham's approach. If he can, he will upset the bowler, stop him bowling to his length with scorching drives.

Suddenly the bowler is insecure, he tries yorkers, bouncers, slower balls, abandoning everything he knows to get his man. Botham is an anarchic cricketer, destroying order on the field.

There were few people on the ground, few in the press box to see this swashbuckling epic, a more serious innings than those of 1981. Four years ago he smote Australia from one side of the Pennines to the other in a celebration of something rediscovered. On this chilly Wednesday in Taunton he simply belted the Hampshire bowling into river and graveyard. If losing the England captaincy let loose his combative spirit, a winter spent on frozen football fields in Scunthorpe and Yeovil has sharpened Botham's game.

At his best he springs to life on the field, swinging his arms as he walks out to bat. Before an innings he can be sleepy, even grumpy and yet as he takes guard he is alert. Others crackle off the field and concentrate grimly on it. Botham is not inhibited by the lullabies of caution, he pretends not to give a damn.

Moreover, he is more enthusiastic than for eight years. Usually he is reluctant to analyse his cricket lest, in explaining his gift, he might lose it. This month he keeps asking about the Australian bowlers.

BOTHAM THE MAN

A<small>T</small> school Ian Botham ran with a gang which beat up other kids if they did not surrender half-a-crown.

He failed his 11-plus exams deliberately because he didn't want to go to grammar school, where they played rugby, but instead went to Bucklers Mead secondary with his mates.

He didn't think mathematics would be of any use to him and he was right.

At 17, not one of his friends took his cricket seriously, yet at 19 he was a champion.

When else has a great sportsman been so drastically under-estimated by his friends, let alone his enemies? His flatmate Dennis Breakwell thought he might clout a few runs in his black-smith's way, but never imagined he'd take any wickets with those gentle outswingers.

Neither did Viv Richards, Vic Marks, nor this correspondent consider Botham to be a potential international cricketer.

We saw him as a buffoon, a likeable, outrageous fellow whose technical limitations would be exposed in the hard world of pro-fessional cricket.

At first other counties agreed. They loathed Botham's pre-cocity. In Melbourne he'd appeared at the Centenary Test match in 1977 and, though still an obscure cricketer, had paraded him-self as if he were already a star.

No one thought he'd amount to much. He was a bounding youngster on a lucky run. Oh yes! He kept dismissing good crick-eters, but it couldn't last.

In a Benson and Hedges match he bowled Barry Richards with an ill-disciplined delivery. Richards, shocked at his fall to this intemperate youth, turned to Derek Taylor to accuse him of kicking over the stumps from behind.

Three years later, in his first Test match, Botham, after a wild beginning, brought about Greg Chappell's downfall with another dreadful delivery.

Chappell hung his head in horror. To have fallen to such a ball . . .

Certainly England's new all-rounder was a country bumpkin. His luck could not hold – could it?

It did, and for many years. On the field his luck never really deserted him. He's had his moments of failure but he has never been dropped from any team in his life for cricketing reasons.

Even in his darkest moments there remained the hope, encouraged by the (in retrospect) misleading series against Australia in 1981 that he could rescue the team with a miracle. Besides which, of course, it was not luck.

The best poker players get the best cards. Botham's 350 Test wickets and 13 Test centuries are not, and cannot be, flukes. Yet whenever things go wrong the carping about Botham's character and technique returns.

Old cricketers – notably Fred Trueman and Ray Illingworth, reared in a classical and respectful northern tradition – do not envy his earnings. They dislike his approach to the game.

At every level and throughout his career Botham has defied the rules. He plays as if he were an appallingly ill-disciplined club player who's been out on the tiles the previous night.

He rides his luck, trusts his spirit and will not obey the principle of line and length, left elbow up, upon which cricket, with its conservative traditions, rears its young.

And so Botham, underestimated at first, and despite those staggering statistics, continues to be regarded as something of an imposter.

He is compared unfavourably with Gary Sobers, such a polite and brilliant cricketer. He is blamed for England's defeats, because he dominates the game so much that if he plays badly the effect on his team is disastrous.

Moreover, it is said, Botham is so wild that he destroys a team's cohesion.

He is a man, they say, with whom you cannot play. Rather pointedly it is noted that England did well in India without him.

Without Botham's anarchic energy, the traditionalist critics observed, the team could at last play as a team.

Unfortunately, England lost to India this summer, while Botham was serving a suspension after he admitted smoking marijuana in private. He did not, as far as we read, confess to other serious and widespread offences such as adultery or drunken driving.

In truth, this prodigious and maverick cricketer is a player England cannot do without.

It is nonsense to say that he cannot, or will not, fit into a team. It is nonsense to suggest that his lack of discipline spoils a team and undermines the captain.

If Botham is wanting discipline then the fault lies as much with the weakness of his leaders as with him. What on earth is the use of captains and managers if they cannot control their players?

Botham, this audacious 30-year-old, this profligate sportsman, is nevertheless a magnificent cricketer and a courageous competitor.

It is up to the captain and to the team to use his talents wisely, and not to complain that they swamp everyone else.

Captains must realise that Botham's success has depended on his ability not to form habits, not to be predictable. Most of us lose our daring when we become professionals.

Botham did not, and this rare quality is of immense value to a team. Besides underestimating Botham as a cricketer, besides misjudging his brilliance because of his vulgarity, it is easy to underestimate him as a man. He is formidable.

On TV recently he was interviewed by Derek Jameson who, without really appearing to, raised some awkward points.

Botham presented himself to the public as a handsome, humorous man who was prepared to admit with a chuckle that his life had been somewhat spicy. But then you couldn't believe everything you read in the papers and anyway whose business was it but his own?

Graham Greene notes that the world is not so much black and white as black and grey. Botham is misrepresented by the press, but he is adept at manipulating his own image.

Throughout his battles with Lord's he has managed to present himself as if he were a Bonny Prince come to rescue his enslaved people. Here he was, Ian Botham, ruggedly handsome, the champion of the people, fighting the crusty old Right-wingers from the MCC.

Of course, it was all poppycock, but the poppycock is often believed if it is presented with sufficient dash. Botham saw his predicament as one that could be exploited.

He believed, perhaps correctly, that he was more sinned against than sinning.

The other tabloids found it hard to forgive Botham his exclusive and enriching relationship with the *Sun*. They were out to get him. Botham also thought that if Lord's turned upon him he could turn his magnificently orchestrated friendship with the public upon them.

He did not believe they'd dare to ban him – nor did he think they had any grounds. But even if they did, he thought it might not turn out so badly.

What an entrance he could make in August, especially as England lost to India. This might be the second phoenix from the ashes. He hadn't really performed any absolute miracles since 1981, had he? It was time for another.

To a friend of Ian, someone who has known him since he was 13, his rises and falls have been neither surprising nor devastating.

Audacity brings its rewards and its dangers. He's had his fun and his cricket has lit the stage.

But a sadness remains, provoking his friends to feelings of warmth and sympathy. Ian, so gregarious in his youth, has been driven by his notoriety into himself. Quite simply, he is a lonely man, perhaps the loneliest I've ever met.

He hides this well, with his boisterous domination of every bar-room and of every cricket club in the country. But occasionally the frightened little boy emerges, fearing above all else that he will be rejected by his friends.

Botham loves male company – relishes the 'matey' side of cricket.

He enjoyed his charity walk for leukaemia because he was with the lads. He was followed and idolised by kids and could have a few pints of an evening.

He returned to the simple pleasures of his youth, as if he were in a pub playing darts or downing a drink faster than anyone else.

It was not always so easy. On tour he hides in his motel room, watching endless videos, ordering up meals from room service, sleeping. It's not a life conducive to mental well-being.

At Taunton, as captain, he sometimes rang up late at night to invite one of his colleagues over for a chat. He just wanted company, someone who would watch Dire Straits on the video and share a beer. (Significantly, he employs his friend Andy Wither, a sort of Sancho Panza, to be his paid companion and secretary.)

At these times, friends see the Botham they like, not the bullying oaf, not the outrageous cricketer, but the vulnerable man. It is hard not to like Botham when you get to know him, when he stops talking about situations to exploit and people to sue.

He says he might return soon. Maybe he will, though I think he dreads leaving Somerset. This might be naive – perhaps he has lost his innocent enjoyment of Somerset people, perhaps country life and county cricket are no longer enough. Perhaps it is too late. I hope not.

Final Fling

EXCERPTS FROM A PLAY IN PROGRESS

From ACT I

SCENE: *a cricket club dressing room.* HENRY, FISH *and* NICK, *in street clothes, are about to change into their whites.*

HENRY: What's it like out there?

NICK: Dry.

HENRY: Christ . . . the way I feel, I couldn't get my granny out. You good for twenty overs, Fish?

FISH: My back's knackered.

Enter PATE

HENRY: Your back's always knackered. Last time you coughed you said it was TB. Here, Pate, what happened to you last night?

PATE: Early night. I went to bed.

HENRY: Early night? Bed? You'll be darning socks next. I haven't had an early night since I was fourteen.

NICK: It looks like it.

HENRY: Bollocks. I can drink you lot under the table and fight you all single handed. Mind you, I can't bloody bowl any more. Fetch me some breakfast, Pate. Nip down to Mrs Jones and see if she'll do a coffee and some pork pies.

PATE: How many?

HENRY: Seven.

PATE: Blimey!

Exit PATE, *as* JOHN *enters*

JOHN: Anyone fancy a bowl?

HENRY: Ah, morning John, old boy. See Scargill last night? And your mate Wedgie?

JOHN: No, were they here?

HENRY: On TV. Bloody shower. And that Scotsman, whatsis-name, the one who doesn't like the Queen. What's his name?

JOHN: Ian McGregor.

HENRY: That's the bloke. Is that him? I thought he played for Celtic. Bloody moaning as usual, they were. I've never known a whinger achieve anything. I can't understand you, siding with him . . . you're just stirring.

PATE *returns with pork pies*

JOHN: They're helping the weak . . .

HENRY: Balls. They're just buggering the whole thing up. Any-way, since when have communists helped the weak? They keep invading them.

JOHN: No-one's defending Russia. That's the strong crushing the weak, same as everywhere else.

HENRY: They're all trying to get men on Pluto. Here, Pate, these pork pies are green. (*He bites into one.*)

JOHN: Anyone fancy a bowl?

From *ACT II*

SCENE 2: *In the Committee Room. Dark wood panelling lined with old photographs. It is a mess.* MRS YOUNG *is cleaning.* PITT *enters.*

PITT: Morning, Mrs Young.

MRS YOUNG: Morning, Mr Pitt.

PITT: It's a rare morning, is it not?

MRS YOUNG: It was raining earlier.

PITT: Gone now . . . We'll play today. Is Mr Young well?

MRS YOUNG: Arthur, he's only ill when the racing's on.

PITT: God, it's a mess, isn't it? See that bloke over there (*He points to a photograph*) . . . See the feet he had? He used to fill his boots with beer at the end of a day, and drink them in one go if he'd taken a few wickets. I thought, if God had bigger feet I'd better start going to church.

MRS YOUNG: I was brought up on cider. We had a vat. My dad used to leave all the lights on so when he woke up in the middle of the night he could get his pint. There was dead rats in it. That's where the phrase comes from.

PITT: Which phrase?

MRS YOUNG: The one about rats.

PITT: He could eat, too! It was like a trough at lunchtime . . . Not so much of it now – all these diets.

MRS YOUNG: Oh, I tried them. They're no good, not those exercises, Jane Fonda and all that . . .

PITT: And that feller there, Griffith. I asked him for his autograph once. He said 'Sod off, kid, me feet are killing me.'

MRS YOUNG: They can get grumpy. I told 'em once, I said, 'Well, it's only a game.'

PITT: What did they say?

MRS YOUNG: They weren't pleased. That Dobson . . .

PITT: He was a character. Still he had a go . . . 'Half-brained twerps who couldn't run a game of marbles.' He shouldn't really have said that about the committee . . .

Enter ASHTON

ASHTON: Good morning Jeremy.

MRS YOUNG *departs*

PITT: Just talking about Dobson . . . quite a character, he was . . .

ASHTON: Balls. Sentimental hogwash! No bloody good at all. Whisky?

PITT: Not for me.

ASHTON: Living in the past . . . sentiment . . . see the club . . . more money around . . . used to be broken down . . . leaking roofs. Food they wouldn't eat in Borstal . . . coffee that tasted like washing up water – didn't someone swap 'em around once?

PITT: Dobson. No-one noticed for two hours.

ASHTON: Nothing to be proud of. Now look . . . buildings . . . we make money . . . modern, rich . . . growing . . .

PITT: Team's good, too.

ASHTON: Bound to be fights, of course . . . shouldn't expect anything else . . . clash of interests . . .

PITT: Something's been lost along the way. Money isn't everything.

ASHTON: People who say that end up selling encyclopedias . . .

PITT: What's wrong with that? This cut-throat business . . . alright, you have to make profits, but there are other things.

ASHTON: Nonsense . . . We put it on a business footing. Dobson had to go. Your problem is you're too soft; you're a farmer. I'm a businessman. How did the farm go last year?

PITT: We made record profits.

ASHTON: Well, that's the EEC for you.

Enter BILL DAVIS

ASHTON: Good morning, Bill.

DAVIS: Mr Ashton, Jeremy.

PITT: The coffee's fresh.

DAVIS: Thanks.

ASHTON: Staying all day, Bill?

DAVIS: Yes. Mr Watts is good that way.

ASHTON: How is the old boy?

DAVIS: Off playing golf today.

ASHTON: Villain at school . . . turned out well. Give him my regards. And don't forget the meeting tonight. We've booked a room at the Chopping Block for 6.30, and dinner for 8, so we can't bugger about.

DAVIS: I don't suppose we can talk forever.

ASHTON: We've had some good old battles in the past. How long did we go last year, Jerry?

DAVIS: I was there; it took three hours.

ASHTON: Well, there you are; and we didn't even sack anyone, did we?

DAVIS: No.

ASHTON: Anyway, we'd better get cracking promptly. Pull up a chair and join us, Bill.

DAVIS: Might pop in to see if the lads are OK. Back in a few minutes.

Exit DAVIS

ASHTON: He still prefers the dressing room. Doesn't he realise he's changed sides?

PITT: He played a long time. Some of the men he played with are still in the team.

ASHTON: They call him the Third Man – after Philby, you see – a traitor.

PITT: Is it because he's the third on this committee too?

ASHTON: I'd never thought of that. Cricketers are too intelligent these days. Some of them. They've more brains than the General Committee.

PITT: It wouldn't be difficult.

ASHTON: Never let on though, eh? You're called Chip-Pitt, you see. Chip off the old block. Clever.

PITT: And you?

ASHTON: Me? Oh, I don't have one.

PITT: Not AA?

ASHTON: AA?

PITT: Well, it could be your initials, or Automobile Association, I suppose.

ASHTON: Or Alcoholics Anonymous? Clever. All my interests in one! Ha! I wonder who thought that little one up.

SCENE 3: *The dressing room.* CURTIS *alone with a 'ghetto blaster', playing Bob Marley's 'Legend'.*

CURTIS (*singing*): No woman, no cry . . . hey, little sister, don't shed no tears . . . No woman, no cry . . . (*He's very smartly dressed and is organising his immaculate kit into which he slowly changes. He rubs things into himself, creams etc; he hasn't brushed his dreadlocks. Eventually* HENRY *enters.*)

HENRY: Good morning, man.

CURTIS: Ah, General Smuts. Hey . . .

HENRY: Pick anything up last night?

CURTIS: Just took it easy . . . Cruised around a little, no problem.

HENRY: Down the pub?

CURTIS: Man, there's too much lawlessness down there . . . too much lawlessness. Don't hold wi' none of that . . . just picked up a little client and went down to the Club.

HENRY: It's OK for you bachelors.

CURTIS: Don't hold wi' marriage, neither. Don't want no part o' that . . . got two children already, don't want no roots, man . . . 'Buffalo soldier . . . Dreadlock Rasta . . .'

HENRY: Talking of roots . . .

CURTIS: Man, to each his own . . . don't hold wi' none of that neither. I'm a Bible man, I say my prayers.

HENRY: You pick up a bird, take her home, bang buggery out of her, and then say your prayers.

CURTIS: We watched a video . . . Bruce Lee. Just taking it easy, cooling out.

HENRY: You blokes are all the same.

CURTIS: Don't say that man – don't say that.

HENRY: Talked to a bloke last night. Big money for a tour to Johannesburg.

CURTIS: It ain't a matter of dollars, it's a matter of security. I go to your place, General Smuts, and I can't go home.

HENRY: Think about it, man. 250,000 pounds for 3 years . . . It's about . . .

CURTIS: You hear what Richards and Lloyd say? You read Marshall in the paper? They offered Marshall a diamond mine.

HENRY: All right, Curtis. No problem.

CURTIS: No problem, man . . . There ain't never no problem.

Enter DAVIS. CURTIS *goes to lie down to sleep or to read the paper*

DAVIS: Can I have a word with you, Henry?

HENRY: Certainly, Bill.

They slide towards a corner

DAVIS: I just had a chat with Taylor.

HENRY: John, you mean?

DAVIS: He's a difficult bastard. I asked for his views on the club policy, and he said he wanted a two year contract. Nothing else.

HENRY: What else is there?

DAVIS: Our contracts meeting – it'll be difficult.

(CURTIS *has put on headphones and the music is gone*)

HENRY: Well?

DAVIS: Look, we played together . . . I'm on your side . . .

HENRY: Yeah . . . Great times. Remember those birds in Darlington?

DAVIS: Aside from that . . .

HENRY: Hard to forget.

DAVIS: Easier if you try . . . Look, Henry we're old mates . . . we're in this together . . .

HENRY: Did you say that to Taylor?

DAVIS: He said something about that's why he'd given up rugby. What can I do? There's going to be trouble.

HENRY: It's simple Bill – you take the players' side.

DAVIS: Someone'll get sacked.

HENRY: Not while I'm around.

DAVIS: There's no choice.

HENRY: There's always choice.

DAVIS: You're not making it any easier. Shall we keep Fisher or Thomas? That's what it'll come down to.

HENRY: Both. I'll fight.

DAVIS: Your benefit's due.

HENRY: What the hell's that got to do with it?

DAVIS: I'm speaking as your friend. They know your troubles. You need 70,000 pounds . . . your gambling. They'll call your bluff.

HENRY: Christ, you're a . . . just fuck off, Bill, just fuck off.

DAVIS: I'll do what I can . . . I'm just warning you. I don't want to spoil things.

(Lights down. Lights up. Same room. Team readying itself to field. A bell rings.)

JOHN: For whom the bell tolls.

CLIFF: (*Popping his head into the room*) We're on our way, lads.

(This does not provoke an enthusiastic response)

NICK: Hey lads, Cliff had a few last night, so keep appealing or else he'll doze off. He might give us a few today. Remember what Dobson said when Cliff gave him out three yards down the pitch? He said, Cliff's a great lad, but he'll have to go! Have to go! Ten years ago that was, ten years.

HENRY: Everyone ready?

NICK: What about our team-talk?

HENRY: What about it?

NICK: We must have a team-talk. It's the best part of the day.

HENRY: You give it. I'm too tired.

NICK: Right . . . Team-Talk. Now then lads this is it, the big one. Get stuck in. This is a vital game. This is a line and length wicket. Bowl line and length. Keep awake in the field. If we win we jump from 12th to 9th in the league. That'd be nice, wouldn't it? (*Players are reading papers, drinking tea, etc.* PATE *is listening.*) Fight 'em at the beaches. Bend ya back, Fish.

FISH: It's buggered . . . gardening.

NICK: Randy old sod . . . you'd screw a barge, that's your problem. Pate, bowl straight, for Christ's sake . . . Curtis . . . will someone wake Curtis up? . . . Bowl your quick stuff, not those leg breaks . . . Everyone ready? Over the top. All aboard . . . shall we go . . . are you coming? C'mon lads, let's go.

(Wearily, they get up and trudge towards the field.)

SCENE 4: *The grandstand.*

ASHTON, PITT *and* DAVIS *are watching the game*

ASHTON: Fill me up, Bill, will you? Might make the nonsense out there go away.

PITT: It's a slow pitch.

ASHTON: Oh, it's not that . . . It's the second-last day, isn't it. They aren't trying.

PITT: It's cold. Hope Mrs Jones hasn't done salad again.

ASHTON: Archer might at least get his hands out of his pockets. I don't know what the sponsors will think. They're paying 1,000 pounds for this.

PITT: It was different in the final wasn't it? Some of them hardly dared watch. I didn't, as a matter of fact.

ASHTON: It was always under control . . . why isn't Archer bowling?

PITT: His shoulder's sore.

DAVIS: It's moved, then.

ASHTON: Pardon?

DAVIS: It was his stomach this morning. 17,000 pounds a year we're paying him . . . 57 wickets . . . 300 pounds a wicket. I hardly got paid that much for a season. Never had my hands in my pockets . . . no respect . . .

ASHTON: Nothing at stake.

DAVIS: I never loafed around . . . we'd have been sacked.

ASHTON: We're more realistic now. If they do their jobs . . .

DAVIS: Look at them . . . no respect . . . it's not right . . .

ASHTON: You can't stop it. Who's going to tell Archer what to do?

DAVIS: See the example he's setting? Hands in pockets.

PITT: Last rule we made we said they had to wear ties. Two of 'em turned up in straw hats, and then someone wore shorts. Archer wore a tie but no shirt. Bloody silly rule.

ASHTON: Because we couldn't enforce it . . . couldn't make it stick. Not while they're winning cups. When Archer goes, we'll have ties then.

DAVIS: It's a shame . . . it's a bloody shame.

ASHTON: A cup's been won, the bills are paid . . .

PITT: Bill's been paid?

ASHTON: The daily ones, not the big ones.

PITT: Oh, I see.

ASHTON: I'd better go and entertain the sponsor. With any luck they'll be pissed by now and won't care the cricket's so bloody awful. Who are the sponsors?

PITT: Maloney, Patterson and Manchee.

ASHTON: Percy Manchee?

PITT: Doesn't say. They're management consultants.

ASHTON: That'll be Percy. It's OK, he hates the game. Used to row at school. Funny bloke, queer as a cart. Married a lovely girl. She only found out when they got married . . . he'd told her he was Catholic. Percy!

PITT: Sounds a nice fellow.

ASHTON: Terrible, really. Better go and see him . . . coming?

PITT: No thank you.

DAVIS: No.

ASHTON: See you later, then.

Exit ASHTON

DAVIS: It'll be quieter now.

PITT: It does look cold out there.

DAVIS: We had a secretary once who said we were too miserable on the field. We said we felt miserable. He said it was putting people off, told us to cheer up. So Dobson and Nick Thomas went around with grins fixed on their faces. Everyone thought they'd gone mad. This was years ago – Dobson did handstands and things. In the end they had him in for drinking on the field. He said he'd been told to enjoy himself, and they said they'd not meant to enjoy himself but to look as if he was enjoying himself.

PITT: No wonder they – we – sacked him.

DAVIS: Yes . . . and what's he doing now? D'you know? Out of work. No job . . . unemployed at 30. What chance have you got? He didn't have anything else, you see, no more than I have. D'you suppose I didn't hate those rules? Those loud committees. I bit my lip. Ask Dobson if it was worth it. He'd not do it again.

PITT: Oh, he would, you know, tomorrow and the day after.

DAVIS: I'm a survivor; no pride, you see. I fit in, do what I'm asked . . . machine man . . . never caused a ruffle; nice house, wife, kid, car. You bite your lip for that. They asked me to roll the pitch once, so I did. And I tipped the forelock. It's how you survive.

PITT: Who's been hurt the most, I wonder: you, or Dobson?

DAVIS: Whose family's been hurt the most? He'd no right, Dobson, I told him . . . warned him . . . disaster waiting to happen . . . had to go . . . wouldn't play the game . . . never quiet.

PITT: If we'd had more like him we'd have changed.

DAVIS: A few would've gone to the wall, first, and I'd have been one . . . No, Jerry. I'm not as . . . cheap as I appear. Not as stupid. I couldn't have survived this long if I'd been stupid. No-one's been in the club longer.

PITT: But you retired early, too early. You had years left. I didn't understand why . . .

DAVIS: Fear. I saw myself slipping. I was offered a job out of the blue, too good to turn down.

PITT: Who by?

DAVIS: A friend . . . of Ashton. He bought me . . . Oh, I know . . . he's got me . . . pitch it up lad, pitch it up . . . why doesn't someone tell him. He's a kid – someone should be telling him . . . used to talk cricket day and night . . . learned your trade that way . . . no training now, no apprenticeship . . . sink or swim. I feel sorry for Pate; what chance has he got? Paid a lot . . . self-destructive. The more you're paid, the better you have to be. It's better not to be paid too much till you're sure of yourself . . . sure of yourself . . .

PITT: Think I'll have a whisky . . . fix one up for you?

DAVIS: A pint . . . I'll have a pint.

SCENE 5: *The cricket field. Only* CLIFF, *the umpire, is visible. A voice from off stage quotes Henry V:*

> . . . there is none of you so mean and base
> That hath not noble lustre in your eyes.
> I see you stand like greyhounds in the slips,
> Straining upon the start.

Lights down. Lights up to reveal NICK, HENRY *and* JOHN *in a staggered slips formation. All crouch alertly except for* HENRY *who has his hands in his pockets.*

NICK (*Loudly*): Oh, well bowled Fish, bad luck mate, next time, next time.

HENRY (*Loudly*): Come on Fish, bend your back. You've got 'im.

JOHN (*Quietly*): Lucky sod.

NICK: Christ, Fish'll never get this bloke out.

HENRY: I couldn't get my granny out on this fucking wicket.

JOHN: He's a lucky bastard.

NICK: Maybe it'll rain.

HENRY: It never rains.

JOHN: Not when you want it to.

(They prepare again. HENRY *doesn't move.* JOHN *shakes his head)*

NICK: Bloody close.

HENRY: He must have a fucking round bat.

JOHN: This bastard is a lucky bastard and that's that.

NICK: See any crumpet anywhere?

HENRY: By the scoreboard.

NICK: In white?

JOHN: How could one bloke have that much luck?

NICK: I'll have the one in pink, big tits.

(They prepare. Nothing happens)

HENRY: You wouldn't chuck her out.

JOHN: No-one ever bowls that rubbish to me.

NICK: I've never chucked anyone.

HENRY: Not the wife?

NICK: Oh, that's different.

(They prepare again, then watch the ball evidently whistling to the boundary)

NICK: It's going to be a long day.

HENRY: What time's lunch?

JOHN: Maybe it'll rain.

NICK *(Loudly)*: Come on Fish, into 'em!

HENRY *(Loudly)*: Big effort, Fish!

FISH *(Off)*: Fuck off!

HENRY: What time's lunch?

JOHN: 1.15. It's curry.

HENRY: Oh, that'll sort out my stomach.

Temporary Blackout
(When the lights come up again, the slips are facing the other way. FISH *is there, between* JOHN *and* HENRY.*)*

FISH: Christ, I'm knackered.

NICK: I think you'll get him in a minute. It's swinging.

FISH: I'm knackered, the ball's like a lump of lard, the pitch is slow and Cliff's asleep. That was plumb.

NICK: Not missing leg?

FISH: Missing leg! Were you watching? Missing leg? It might have missed the leg and it might have missed off, but it bloody well would have taken middle. Cliff's asleep.

HENRY: You're bowling great, Fish. Feeling strong, good for a few more?

FISH: Bloody marvellous, Captain. Me ankles ache, me shins are sore, shoulder hurts. That was plumb, you know.

HENRY: Bloody close, anyway. You're bowling terrific.

FISH: Oh, thanks.

HENRY: Try a couple more, and then have a blow.

FISH: Oh, it's all right. I'll keep going. Some bastard's got to bowl. They ought to dig up this pitch, though.

HENRY: No bloody good at all. It's a shit heap.

NICK (*Loudly*): Come on Pate, into it!

FISH (*Loudly*): Let's go Pate, you can get 'im, lad!

HENRY: It's bloody hard bowling into the wind.

FISH: It's bloody hard bowling down the wind.

(A crack – four runs)

NICK: Good shot, that. Field's wrong. Need some more blokes out there; too many bloody slips.

HENRY (*Loudly*): Curtis, man, move a shade over dat way, will ya?

NICK: It's going to rain, you know. It's building.

HENRY: So is Stonehenge.

NICK: A fiver says it rains by noon.

FISH: Done.

HENRY: It's fucking spitting now.

FISH: Spitting doesn't count.

NICK: Why not?

FISH: Rain means rain stops play. I'd hardly bet against it spitting when it's spitting, would I?

NICK: You've been backing No. 4 in the Grand National for 13 years.

FISH: Well, it will win one day.

HENRY: It's going to piss down.

FISH: Never tempt the fates.

NICK: Don't watch the clouds. A watched pot never boils.

HENRY: Eh?

NICK: A watched pot – well, you know what I mean.

FISH: He means it will rain if we pretend it isn't going to. But if we think it's going to, it won't.

(The others stare at him – this is a rare flash of brilliance.)

FISH: They never taught me that at school. They seemed to think rain had something to do with clouds.

JOHN: And what caused clouds?

FISH: Well, I don't know, they just gather.

JOHN: From where?

FISH: From all over the place. They just form.

JOHN: From little bits to big bits?

FISH: Yes, that's it. That's right.

JOHN: Where do the little bits come from?

FISH: Christ, I don't fucking well know. But it's got bugger-all to do with whether we're watching them, that I do know.

(They settle for a ball. A hit is heard.)

JOHN: Straight into a fucking gap.

HENRY: I just moved him from there. Whose idea was that?

NICK: Mine!

HENRY: Well, you're a bastard.

FISH (*Loudly*): Bad luck, Pate! Come on son!

HENRY (*Loudly*): Keep going, Pate!

JOHN: Yes.

FISH: See the soccer last night?

NICK: Hoddle's a poof.

FISH: He scored a goal.

NICK: He pranced around like he's got a sticky bun up his backside.

HENRY (*Calling out*): Here, Cliff, isn't it raining up your end? What about the bloody rain, then?

CLIFF: Hang on a few minutes, Skip. Got to make it look right.

HENRY: Cliff's gone mad.

(*They settle.* HENRY *drops a catch.*)

HENRY: Shit! Bollocks! Bugger it!

NICK: Bad luck, Skip.

HENRY: Just got it in my left hand. Didn't get it right. Fuck it! Bloody thing popped out. Balls! It dipped at the end. Saw it all the way, you know. Couldn't catch a cold these days.

FISH: I'd have caught that between the cheeks of my arse.

HENRY: Here Cliff, this ball's like a bar of soap. If we stay out here we'll catch a cold.

CLIFF (*Off*): Great stop, Captain. Good stop that. As a matter of fact, my arthritis is beginning to play up. Gentlemen, I think we'll leave the field.

HENRY: Thank Christ for that. That's more like it, Cliff. I thought you'd cracked for a minute. Let's go, lads.

PEOPLE

SAMMY WOODS

WHO is the only man to have played Test cricket for Australia without ever playing a first-class game here? Another clue? He played Rugby for England 15 times and was once asked to play an Ashes Test in Sydney but caught a cold in a Turkish bath the night before and had to withdraw.

Samuel Moses James Woods was his name. Sportsman, fisherman and a hunter who said he'd shot hounds and keepers in his time – he was probably joking – Woods was a mixture of English rural gentry and Australian pugnacity.

Woods was born in Ashfield, Sydney, and attended Royston College on the North Shore. His father, a businessman and grazier, had a large family, 14 or so Sam reckoned, though he wasn't particular about numbers. The boys played cricket and boxed with the local Aboriginal champion, who knelt to fight them.

At 13 young Sam was sent to England to become a proper gentleman, a distinction he resisted gamely. He played soccer as a goalkeeper for Brighton College but settled in Bridgwater, Somerset, with a chum of his father's and played skittles, billiards, Rugby, soccer and cricket for the county besides being the life and soul of things.

Being a gentleman, Woods duly applied to go to Oxford. Now Sam had many qualities; he could sing Cockney songs in a light baritone, he could turn a lady's eye and he could drink rough cider with the best. But he was not blessed with grey matter. For a start his spelling was atrocious. Oriel College rejected him. Later, when Sam was running riot in university contests with Oxford's deadly enemies, Oriel protested that no-one had told them this Woods fellow played cricket. They scoured the city for someone to stand up to him and eventually gave a scholarship to the son of a local hairdresser, whose spelling was no more accurate than Sam's.

Cambridge took him. Just. Latin was required. At his interview Sam was asked if he'd heard of Julius Caesar. Yes, sir. Know anything about him? No, sir. What did he do? . . . Wrote books, sir. What about? . . . Some place called Gaul. What happened in Gaul? . . . They fought battles, sir. So what was Caesar? . . . A soldier, sir.

It was enough. Passing exams was another matter. When Sam approached his examinations the whole university went with him. A giant figure with a shock of thick hair and wearing a tatty gown, Woods was morose on these occasions. Few fancied his chances. Inside the Corn Exchange rooms he'd bite his pen and write precious little. After a few minutes he'd wander out crestfallen.

It is said that on one paper he wrote only S. M. J. Woods, Jesus College, and that one word had been misspelt. From this slender evidence the examiners detected sufficient learning to allow Woods his full term, a widely popular judgement.

Finally Woods returned to Bridgwater to live in a local pub and to play outstanding cricket as an amateur. To most amateurs cricket was about art not sweat. They were batsmen. Woods would have none of this nonsense. Life was too short for such pomposity. He did both. As a batsman he hit booming drives and called loudly for perilous singles his partners did not always complete.

Bowling was his strength. As a fast bowler he mixed them up because to him a cove wasn't bowling if he merely let go of the ball.

Woods had a deadly slower one, unflagging imagination and enough skill to play regularly for the Gentlemen versus Players.

Pretty soon Woods was a giant in the county, winning Rugby caps and hunting stags. In 1888 he played three Tests for the Australian tourists, replacing S. P. Jones who'd contracted smallpox.

In his time he captained Somerset, a task he carried out with the requisite humour. For years he carried the side upon his mountainous back, playing heroically and never losing heart. Great-heart was one of his nicknames. Preparing to bat on a bad pitch once he sat enjoying a double whisky and soda and a Burmese cheroot. A wicket fell. 'This must stop,' he bellowed and promptly smote his first three balls over midwicket. He hit 70.

Another time, encountering a dishonest umpire, he told him:

'In 20 years it won't matter who won the game to anyone except you.'

Often he used to walk to games, tramping along miles of country roads, stopping to talk to the farmers. When in company he would sometimes dart behind a tree and produce a bottle of beer which he had hidden for just such an emergency. A noted raconteur and after-dinner speaker, Woods could recite from memory the long verses locals wrote to celebrate the county's rare victories.

Sammy never did get to take life seriously. He did try, once, to learn a trade, giving a surveyor 50 pounds to instruct him in the mysteries of roods and perches. After one lesson the fellow went home and shot himself. Woods used to say, 'It wouldn't be expedient for anyone to pay me for measuring a plot of ground.' A bachelor, he was reputed to have a bit of fluff in town but generally spent his time playing snooker in the clubs.

He returned once to Australia. Twenty years he'd been away. His family met him on the dock. With his walloping stride Woods disembarked. It was a moment of high emotion. Woods gazed around, saw his family and moved towards them. Then he stopped, pulled out his pipe, walked up to his father and said, 'Hello Guv'nor, got a light?'

Crippled by arthritis, Woods finally stopped playing and took to administering, at which he was hopeless. He stayed in Somerset, his voice bellowing across grounds until he went the way of all flesh. He died practically unknown in Australia but all Somerset attended his funeral.

WHATEVER HAPPENED TO OTTO NOTHLING?

'WHATEVER happened to Otto Nothling?' a friend asked over dinner a while ago. Otto Nothling? Couldn't place the fellow at all. Perhaps he was a warlike saint from medieval Germany given to riding into town to rescue maidens from marauding Huns. Plainly, a library visit was in order.

Otto, it has emerged, was a man of far greater distinction than any mere saint, for he was the only fellow for whom Donald Bradman was ever dropped. Accordingly, I have an idea. As Adelaide's cricket ground moves reluctantly towards an age for which it does not much care, its stretched concertina shape suggesting it be renamed the Adelaide Oblong, a stand has been dedicated to the greatest of all batsmen, Don Bradman. What about a stand for poor old Otto? Imagine it, being picked ahead of Bradman! Who was this fellow?

Otto's origins were suitably colourful. His parents were Germans who fled to Australia in 1870 after supporting the wrong side in the Franco–Prussian War. Otto's father had left behind a rich estate, just outside Berlin, and a life of plenty, to begin again in a new land.

Penniless, their university degrees unrecognised, the Nothlings survived in Australia by making bricks, later clearing a forest to build a farm. Otto was born in Witta, in the Blackall Ranges of South East Queensland, in 1900. The youngest of eight children, he was sent to Brisbane Grammar, the family fortunes having revived somewhat thanks to hard work, and then to university in Sydney because he was to be a medical student and Queensland had no medical college. Otto was the brightest of the children and in time it would be up to him to support his family.

Otto quickly made an impact on university life. Standing six foot three inches (190.5 cm) in his socks he was a powerful, fit and gregarious man who could run the 100 yards in even time and jump like a kangaroo. Duly chosen to represent Sydney in the University Games he was, out of the blue, asked to throw the javelin. Things were tight in the competition and even token points would be important. Otto had never seen a javelin before and upon hearing that practice throws were not allowed asked if he could go last so as to observe his rivals. Casting an eye over the javelin, he pronounced it a pretty good spear of the sort he'd used for sticking pigs on his farm back home, whereupon he proceeded to break the NSW, Australian and Australasian records with his first throw.

Professor Cotton later put this feat down to Nothling's habit of hurling stones across a chasm while tending cattle on the farm. He never threw the javelin again because he found it too dull. Otto was also an outstanding Rugby player, playing for the Waratahs – effectively the Australian XV – against the Maoris and against South Africa. He was a fullback who, according to Herbert Moran, 'had every attribute for becoming the greatest footballer ever, except one: intuition'. Otto was a safe player who made his moves after careful calculation, one who never allowed his unconscious mind to take over. Fearing injury, he gave up the game at 24 and later advised his son, also a doctor, to do the same.

But cricket was Otto's first love. It wasn't unusual for families from Northern Europe to play cricket in Queensland. In 1928 Kann, Olehmann and Oelkers represented Toowoomba, while Frauenfelder and Steinhort played for Queensland Country. Accordingly, after finishing his studies, Nothling began to work his way from grade cricket to the Shield team.

Otto was a zestful medium pacer who, according to Bill Brown, used his height to nip the ball off the wicket. Brandishing a heavy bat he feared no bowler and was good enough to score 121 against New South Wales in Sydney in 1929–30.

Otto was duly chosen to represent Queensland against Percy Chapman's 1928–29 tourists, seizing his opportunity by taking five wickets for 78, including those of Sutcliffe, Hammond, Tyldesley, Chapman and Ames – the cream of English batting.

Then Australia, despite a brave innings of 30 by Woodfull, lost the first Test ever played in Brisbane by 675 runs, a youngster called Bradman batting at seven and utterly bemused by a wet pitch of a sort never encountered in Bowral scoring 18 and one. Plainly changes had to be made. Obviously this new lad Bradman had been promoted prematurely and must be dropped. Australia's selectors were, that year, a curious bunch, given to consulting little black books crammed with statistics rather than the evidence of their eyes. Already they had recalled ageing spinner Bert Ironmonger (46), and now they summoned his 49-year-old club mate, Don Blackie. Jack Gregory, wonderful and charismatic cricketer, had been injured in Brisbane and sadly his career was over. Gregory limped into the English dressing room 'a picture of misery', said Patsy Hendren, and sighed: 'Boys, I'm finished. Never again shall I bowl you out.' Tears were streaming down his face. Kelleway had suffered from food poisoning, and he too was dropped. Besides Blackie, Vic Richardson and Otto Nothling were picked for the second Test in Sydney.

He didn't do badly, really. In his first over he rapped Jack Hobbs and Herbert Sutcliff on the pads, and wasn't game to appeal because it was, in those days, considered poor form to shout unless it was plumb. Later the umpire said he'd have ruled for the bowler on both occasions. Hobbs and Sutcliffe scored hundreds and, to the dismay of 170,109 people, Australia lost again.

In his pomp Nothling used to chuckle and say it could all have been so different, for he was a wet wicket specialist and, as it happened, the following Test in Melbourne was played on a rain-affected pitch. Spectators were more sanguine, one advising his neighbour to cast an eye over this Nothling because he'd never be seen again. Otto didn't deserve that, but luckily he had a broad sense of humour and decades later he was accustomed to beginning lectures by introducing himself as the only fellow who had ever turfed Bradman out of a cricket team.

In his only Test, Nothling bowled 42 overs and took 0-60 as England strode towards its huge total of 656. Contemporaries recall a tall cricketer banging the ball down at the wide bats of the wise English professionals. He scored 52 runs, adding 101 in 67 minutes with his captain, Jack Ryder. His running between the wickets caused anxiety, and he was eventually run out by Hendren. In his book on the series, Monty Noble observed: 'The athletic Queenslander played a fine fighting knock.'

It wasn't enough and Nothling was dropped. The youngsters Bradman and Archie Jackson were given the chance to claim their kingdom. Nothling returned to Queensland cricket to play a few more games, to bowl to Ponsford when he scored 437 in 621 minutes after Victoria had been put in to bat, to captain his state on three occasions, upon which he retired because he had to support his family and doing so meant taking his practice to Maryborough, 280 km north of Brisbane.

Otto took up golf and was quickly playing off scratch. He was soon the life and soul of the Maryborough community, who regarded him as an eccentric because he was given to driving around in a World War II jeep dressed to the nines in a dark suit and wearing a fedora. During the war he had served in the Red Cross in Egypt and Greece, where he survived several close shaves before being invalided out.

With his limbs failing he gave up his general practice and, at the age of 50, went to Sydney for two years to study for a new career as a dermatologist.

Returning home he was elected president of the QCA and immediately set about ridding Queensland cricket of its cobwebs. He took an interest in district games, and played billiards until dawn with touring players. He was universally beloved in Brisbane cricket. On Saturdays he'd drive around the grade games hoping that cricket was being played properly.

One hot Sunday late in 1965 Otto left the cricket to cut his lawn. Family and friends said it was too hot, but Otto wasn't a man to be deterred by things like that. His heart rebelled. His death was deeply felt. Nothling's first class career brought 882 runs and 36 wickets, and he was, perhaps, lucky to play for his country. Yet, in his way, he was as great a man as ever did play.

THE TOUGH BIT

Trevor King, of Carlingford, in Sydney's central west, is one of sport's most extraordinary men. Consider the bare facts. He was born in 1930. His father was an alcoholic, as were six of his nine brothers.

At 11, both Trevor's legs and one arm were paralysed by polio; yet at 23, he was featherweight boxing champion of Australia. That year a dreadful motorcycle accident scuppered a world title bout; but refusing a leg amputation, King was back walking again in 2½ years, and fighting in six.

He carried on until hepatitis and another accident led to his retirement at 30. A colourful period was followed by an incredible conversion to religion and to missionary work.

He sits now, looking rather like George Bush surrounded by sparring gloves, counselling the bereaved, the suicidal, the derelict and the emotionally or sexually disturbed.

No author would dare write such a script. King was the last of 13 children, born in the depression years into a hard-drinking, brawling family which farmed land near the mining town of Cessnock. Despite malnutrition and poverty all ten brothers were good local boxers.

Only Trevor, bespectacled, constantly reading, and immobile, could not fight. Then, sitting in a wheelchair, he heard a brother say that Leo, the second youngest, was the family's last hope for a title.

'Is that so?' thought Trevor, and at once vowed, although he could not walk, to be a champion.

'We have the power,' he says now, 'to change our lives. There is no need for anyone to struggle under the burden of negativity. What a man can conceive he can do.'

Luckily, Taff Thomas, an outstanding trainer with 'healing in his hands', lived in Cessnock and accepting this unpromising juvenile candidate, began to massage life into his limbs.

Propped up on a tripod, King learned to use his right to defend and to counter-punch, and when his body was finally cured he had fast quicksilver hands. His footwork, in contrast, appeared plodding, which lulled opponents into a false security.

King was scientific, economical, superbly fit, and devastating. In his early Cessnock fights King's opponents would roar with laughter upon seeing his boney body. On top of everything else he was a vegetarian, telling appalled trainers 'when I start losing fights I'll start eating steak'.

In his career, he lost only one of his 61 contests, and was decked just once. Always he fought to win and with no fear of defeat.

At 16, King fought Rex 'Tommy' Jackson, later State Minister for Corrective Services, and later still, like many of King's past and present friends, a prisoner.

King had heard the Jacksons were cunning, so he was not surprised when Rex hurtled across the ring as the bell rang. A fast right planted Jackson on the canvas, and the fight was stopped after two seconds.

A lot of money had been gambled and lost on the bout, about which Jackson's recollections are hazy.

These were great days for Australian boxing, with roaring crowds packing into 'The Old Tin Shed' at Rushcutters Bay to see champions like Vic Patrick, Dave Sands and Tommy Burns.

But corruption was also rife, with criminals trying to bribe boxers to throw fights. Two men used to contact King, asking for his predictions. After the fights they would give him a wad of notes. Only later did he realise they assumed he was fixing his fights to fulfil his forecasts and their bets.

Rising through the ranks, King now met Elley Bennett, the great Aboriginal champion, with whom he'd unknowingly sparred as a kid when Bennett turned up unheralded at his gym. By now Bennett was a shadow of his former self and had not King been suffering terribly from an injection of penicillin, to which it emerged he was allergic, he'd have won on a knockout.

Years later he heard Bennett had been arrested for drunkenness for the umpteenth time and tried to help. But Elley was 'a mountain of blubber. The grog had got him. He had never done a foul thing in his life.'

By 1954 King was in line for a world title fight in America which he expected to win. Then came a dreadful motorcycle accident. Gangrene set in, and an eminent surgeon wanted to amputate. King told him never to appear at his bedside again. Determined to walk, and fight, again, he worked all day every day in the gym.

He discharged himself after 12 months and threw away his crutches. He was walking within 2½ years, and at 30 was back in the ring, beating New Zealand lightweight champion Mike Corless in five rounds.

Unbelievably, fate was not yet finished with King, for now he caught hepatitis and was in a second dreadful accident which left him concussed and with amnesia. Someone, evidently, didn't want him to fight on, so he retired.

Abandoning, temporarily, his ascetic life of dedicated training King took to gambling, smoking and drinking until, sitting alone one dark wintry morning in a Parramatta church, King obliged 'the religious ratbags' trying to convert him by closing his eyes and muttering: 'Well, God, this is your chance – do something.'

No clap of thunder followed. He opened his eyes scornfully and saw an ethereal light on the altar. Following it, drawn by it, he moved to a wall that read in bright letters: 'Be still and know I am God.'

God had done something.

This was not King's only mystical experience. In Lebanon he was saved from shrapnel by a bible which he'd just inexplicably moved from left to right breast pocket.

Again, when boarding a helicopter in Cyprus, he was pulled aside by a priest. He can still feel the tug on his arm. A minute later a missile brought down the helicopter, killing everyone aboard. No-one else saw the priest.

It reminded King of a pugilistic Catholic pastor of his youth, Father Lloyd, who'd told him: 'The Lord has great and wonderful things for you to do. Be alert when he calls.'

Parramatta was enough. Converted, King first joined the Salvation Army and then, seeking independence, formed his own mission.

Working from Carlingford he counselled the bereaved from the Granville train disaster. He rushed off to help suicidal teenagers. He dowsed himself in methylated spirits, dressed for the part, and mixed with downtown derelicts.

Squabbling spouses and prisoners are visited, those addicted to drugs assisted. To these victims King repeats his positive philosophy: 'Get rid of the mask, get rid of the past, be the person you have it in you to be.'

To Trevor King, people, not drugs, are the problem. He says government campaigns against drugs are a mistake because they magnify by concentration. Alternatives, like work and sport, are needed.

Already he is building a 35-hectare farm in the bush to provide such an alternative. Always he searches for the positive.

King now lives in a modest home with his wife and children. He tells his family to ignore newspaper stories of his brave deeds – like pulling a body from a blazing car, rescuing a pensioner from assailants and saving a child from oncoming traffic.

True courage, says King, lies in 'facing up to life and living morally. That is the tough bit'.

STILL THE GREATEST

Last week Muhammad Ali was in Lahore, staying at the same hotel as England's cricketers. In his career he enjoyed a huge following among Muslim sportsmen in Pakistan, but he had never previously visited the country. His trip was sponsored, to the tune of $50,000, by a Lahore building firm.

His programme was hectic. He paid homage at a Muslim shrine, prayed in a mosque and met the chief minister of the Punjab (who, this being a one-party state, opened the batting against England next day).

Later, Ali visited Afghan refugees, watched a bout of Pakistani wrestling, waved, shook hands and kissed babies, while issuing statements condemning drugs, praising the mujaheddin and declaring his willingness to die for Islam. Ali's magic worked well, as the crowds flocked to him, clapping and cheering. All appeared in order.

Sadly, the truth was very different. Ali's fellow hotel guests saw the sombre and terrible truth, as boxing's most articulate champion shuffled (a poignantly ironic verb) from lobby to room, occasionally shadow-boxing, still pumping hands, scarcely uttering a word, as if his brain was dying in an insidious and impenetrable fog.

His dedicated entourage (all black) followed him, guided him, usually spoke for him and sometimes propelled him around hotel and city. Suffering from Parkinson's syndrome, a legacy of those brutal fights in the 1970s, Ali is facing the toughest challenge of his extraordinary career. Punch-drunk, he is now fighting for his life against a remorseless enemy.

Those who revered Ali in his prime were moved by the fortitude with which Ali carried out his duties. Broken but not bent, he has not retreated from the limelight to live in decent obscurity, hiding his decline from adoring fans. Certain of his faith, hugging his public, possibly needing the money and aware that he is dying, Ali has nevertheless insisted on facing his public. He continues to shuffle. In his way, he is still majestic. A big man undone by sickness. You can be a temporarily great sportsman, but you cannot be temporarily a great man.

CHEE QUEES

Scan the Randwick first grade batting order, and for a time all is well, Banwell opening with Harris. Then things go haywire, for Chee Quee is listed next. It must be a misprint. Sanity returns with Millican and Peck, only for Chee Quee to return at No. 6. No-one, you see, has told Richard and Michael Chee Quee that Chinese can't play cricket.

Richard, 18, has played for NSW under-19s these past two years, and he bats first drop for his club. Big and powerful, he has long black hair, smokes, wears a vest, and altogether resembles one of those fellows who grabs a machete and chases you after you've forgotten to pay for your sweet-and-sour. Michael, 21, was State junior handball champion of 1986–87, and bats at 6. He is smaller, brighter, smarter, and has spiky hair. He looks like one of those who were squashed in Tiananmen Square. They live with their mother, grandmother and sundry relations (so it appeared) in a decorous long house in a wide Kingsford street.

So how do two Chinese lads take to cricket? Actually they hardly know anything about being Chinese, and couldn't even pin down the Chinese New Year though they'd plainly just cele-brated its Australian equivalent. Mother arrived, bringing a pile of steamed pork buns, and said 'Oh, they're more Western than Asian', then took up the tale herself.

Granddad had moved to Thursday Island, above Cape York Peninsula, raising a family of 13 and opening a store to service merchant ships on their way to Australian docks. Mother, a mixture of Chinese and Fijian, one of a dozen siblings and a lady with five languages at her command, including Mandarin and Cantonese, took a holiday on the island. The rest is the province of violins.

Soon the newlyweds settled in Sydney's Kensington and opened a fish shop hard by the Doncaster Hotel, an immensely popular meeting-place for locals. The fish shop was popular, too, the Chee Quees being hospitable folk, until it was blown up when a Lebanese outfit which ran an adjoining furniture shop used too much explosive in its quest for insurance money.

Born and bred in Sydney, the Chee Quees took up sport as tots, playing with gusto in their backyard. 'How many windows,' Mrs Chee Quee laments, 'have been broken since then.' Skilled at league, tennis and soccer, cricket was nevertheless their pride and joy and the brothers urged each other on as they rose through the ranks of junior and school cricket, helping Marcelin College, where their education was strict, to win the Catholic Schools Cup for the first time in 22 years.

Soon enough Michael forced his way into Randwick's first grade team. The remarks were made, of course, about his origins but Michael smiles in remembrance, recollecting nothing untoward, besides which the experience added to his determination to prove he could play cricket.

Richard laughs, too, and says no-one bothers him now, which, considering his size, is hardly surprising. Both were steeled by a desire to show they did belong on the cricket field.

Richard made his first grade debut at 16, scoring 52 not out against Wayne Daniel, and he has been Randwick's leading scorer this year. Last week he struck 136 in 100 balls in an under-21 game against Western Suburbs.

Michael has been less happy with his form. Not that Richard is content either, having recently returned from Adelaide where he failed to win selection for Australia's under-19 team, batting below his best. Disarmingly he confessed: 'We had a fortnight to make our mark. Maybe I just cracked under the pressure.'

Asking each of the pair how his brother batted recaptured the backyard scraps of their early days. Richard growled: 'If you say, "He's a slogger", I'll kill you.' Michael tried 'unorthodox' and Richard, pained, asked: 'You reckon I'm unorthodox?' Seeking safer waters, Michael concluded: 'He's aggressive, though he's calmed down a bit now he's first drop. He has an exceptional eye and loves to hook fast bowlers.'

For his part Richard said Michael played spinners well and was strong off his pads, an analysis which astounded his brother who stoutly maintained a preference for fast bowlers and driving. A compromise being reached, it emerged that Michael was a correct dasher.

Certainly both are dedicated to cricket. 'Once you play to a high status,' said Michael, 'you want to see how far you can go.' Last winter they paid their way to Liverpool, England, to play league cricket. Both did well and Richard broke all manner of records for runs, sixes and hundreds.

Living above a chip shop they were thoroughly spoiled by a Chinese family whose broad Liverpudlian accent amused them enormously though they themselves have a distinctive Aussie twang. They were hugely popular and plan to return this winter to take up professional positions.

These Chee Quees are an entertaining and capable pair who find cricket dull to watch and exciting to play. Chinese, you see, can play cricket; anyone can who wants to enough. Hopefully the Chee Quees will continue to pile on the runs because I want to go back. Those steamed pork buns were delicious.

PETER McWHINNEY

PETER McWhinney, who tees off in the NSW Open at The Lakes tomorrow, is not a conventional golfer. Talking to him is like conversing with Huckleberry Finn's older brother.

McWhinney was raised on a property out the back of Bourke where he trapped birds, galahs and currawees sometimes, with a box, a bit of grain and a piece of string; where he drove cars as an eight-year-old, shot pigs, foxes and snakes, and generally ran wild. Like Mr Finn he had no use for shoes, cutlery, combs or any of those implements which cramp a fellow. Nor had education made a high impression upon him. Asked to name the first president of America, McWhinney, stabbing in the dark, tried 'Batman'.

Seeing her son run free did not worry Mother McWhinney who believed city children had to fit into a conventional strait jacket and preferred her family to find their own personality in the open honesty of bush life. But then Peter, accustomed to stretching authority to its limits, began to run a little too wild, so she sent him to board at Cranbrook School in Sydney, quietly telling the headmaster, Mark Bishop, that if he could teach her son to tie his laces and to use a knife and fork she'd consider her money well spent.

McWhinney took a different view. One glance at the dormitories, books and timetables was enough. Not for him a life of poetry and sums. If this was education he was not having a bar of it, so he upped and headed for home. In his first year he ran away and was brought back regularly.

In time, school and pupil learned to accommodate each other, for they had a humanity in common. If lessons grew dull McWhinney would wander down to the Oval and chat to George Eccles, the curator, about pitch preparation and other fascinating topics. Sometimes he hit a golf ball with a broken scythe until, eventually, someone would fetch him and he'd once more try to remember who followed William and Mary.

Unimpressed by academe, with eyes only for bush tales and Phantom magazines, McWhinney was totally immersed in sport throughout his school life.

Only once did his mother appear at Cranbrook, entering the study with the words: 'It's ruddy hot, ain't it?' whereupon she removed her shoes. Mostly she left Peter to find his own way.

McWhinney decided he wanted to play cricket for Australia as a fast bowler. Cricket was his favourite game; still is, as a matter of fact. He followed Australia's fortunes while playing golf in Europe this winter. With determination and a growing physique he quickly rose to the school first XI and was soon a legendary and feared fast bowler around the campus.

Nor, typically, did he rise by currying favour. Buttering people up wasn't for him, they could take him as they found him.

But then came disillusionment with cricket. McWhinney had taken 10-31 to beat arch rivals Knox who, determined upon vengeance, prepared a spinner's track for the return game, which they duly won. When he was out, McWhinney threw away his bat and gloves and stamped off in high dudgeon.

Nor were things well in Bourke where the drought had forced his family to sell up and return to Brisbane, where McWhinney resumed his cricket career. Sadly, he found little encouragement there, and, frustrated, decided to give cricket away. In 1975, at 19 years of age, he took up golf.

Apart from a few hacks at school, he'd never played the game. On his first round he lost 11 balls and found 14. Determined never to work in an office, dedicated to being a professional sportsman, he found a job in a market which left his afternoons free to practise. Quickly he decided he liked golf. 'You are the sole master out there. If you do it well you get rewarded,' he said.

Starting so late hasn't made it easy for McWhinney. Staying with friends, playing pro-ams, he lived from hand to mouth until 1980 when, slowly, he began to improve. Soon he was earning his keep and in 1985 he tried for his playing card in America, only to three-putt the first play-off hole. Rules were changed in 1986, a year too late, and this failure depressed him. Awoken by his wife, he fought back, went to the European circuit this winter, and regularly finished high in the lists.

He has done it all on his own terms and without ever being asked to recite the kings and queens of merry England.

R. J. O. MEYER –
CAD, GENIUS AND FOX

ALLOW me to tell you about Rollo John Oliver Meyer, my old headmaster, and sometime captain of Somerset. Meyer played for the Gentlemen, was a cotton broker in India, founded a great school in an army camp, was a gambler, golfer, chess player, scholar, scrounger, crossword solver and sundry other things it's too late to be bothered with now.

Born in 1905, son of an impoverished, gentle rector, Meyer learned to live by his wits during the potato famine of his boyhood, shooting swallows for food while his mother, less well informed, fed rhubarb leaves to her backyard hens which all promptly died.

Surviving the rough and tumble of private school life, Meyer was sent to Cambridge where he won his cricket blue, playing beside Kumar Duleepsinhji and under Kiwi Tom Lowry, founder member of the Hellfire Club, to enter which a fellow had to blow three smoke rings and spit through them.

Lowry, a fellow after Meyer's heart, once went to Newmarket races with a £5 note and returned with a small motor car. At dentists he scorned anaesthesia.

Meyer was a dashing batsman and a bowler who had studied at the feet of S. F. Barnes and Monty Noble, masters of spin, curve and change of pace. On leaving Cambridge in 1925, Meyer was still broke, so he went to India in search of his fortune. In 10 years a fellow could grow rich in cotton, so they said.

He did well, surviving the slump, selling cotton by playing cards with the Chinese, giving racing tips to the Greeks and playing pool with locals. He played cricket, too, for various sides, and ruined three pairs of sandshoes while scoring 275 in 35 degree heat, and took 28 wickets in the 1927 quadrangular tournament against Muslim, Hindu and Parsee teams.

Alas, depression dug deep and Meyer, still poor, prepared to sail for home. At the docks he bumped into Ranjitsinhji who, hearing of his plight, arranged for him to educate the charges of a wealthy prince.

Meyer taught 80 pupils, whose ages ranged from nine to 27, in separate rooms on the first floor of a palace. His boss was the laziest man he ever met, being lifted from bed to bath by a machine.

When the prince's son scored 50 for Eton he sent a telegram of congratulation and promised to sacrifice 50 slaves in his honour, a consummation narrowly avoided. Meyer coached many of India's top cricketers, including Amar Singh, the great fast bowler.

Returning to England in 1935, Meyer founded Millfield, in Somerset, a school which started as a crammer and quickly built a reputation for being radical in entry, co-educational, capable of teaching dyslexic children and yet conservative in discipline. Stupid children of aristocrats paid twice so that gifted sons of miners could attend.

Besides playing superb golf, Meyer represented Somerset in his holidays, once scoring 200, and often taking wickets. Had he not concentrated upon education he'd have played for England, so they say.

To cricket he brought his full powers of originality. Facing Bill Bowes's inswingers on a bad track, he announced he must be hit for six over point and promptly played the shot himself first ball.

Bowling to Don Bradman he sent every man to the legside boundary, tried a high full toss and, seeing Bradman hit it between two men, Meyer turned round and called out 'orthodox field please'.

Surprise was his weapon, experiment his fancy, dullness his enemy, inconsistency his weakness.

Meyer played against the greats. Bowling to Harold Larwood he once accidentally sent down a bumper. Larwood raised an eyebrow and said: 'Look after me, Sir, and I'll look after you.' In his turn, Meyer reached 49 and Larwood whispered: 'Sorry Sir, but I'll have to bounce you when you reach 50.'

After the war, in 1947, with a bad disc, lumbago and poor eyesight, Meyer was asked to captain Somerset which was in its customary dire strait. Taking six aspirins a day he did well. One colleague said he was 'a peculiar player, a bit touched. He'd been to India you know.'

Another joke was 'one thing stops him being a great batsman

– he never stayed in longer than five minutes'. They liked his racing tips and his capacity for stopping trains, wandering into town and returning with seven pounds of horse steak for his hungry men in those years of rationing.

Scrupulousness never prevented an idea, once hatched, being applied. Pebbles might appear on a length and once he told his men to take the field after lunch without him and his spinner to deliver a full toss. Instructions followed, the batsman was duly caught by Meyer, emerging belatedly and cunningly from the pavilion shadows.

Gambles were frequent, too. Bowled out for 25 in a local derby, Meyer bet his rival captain £100 that his ageing team would score 400 in its next innings. Joined by Horace Hazell, a rotund spinner, at 9-347, Meyer offered his partner £1 if they made it. At 9-379 Bill Voce was recalled and, sensing Hazell's morale wavering, Meyer marched down the pitch and said: 'I'll make it a fiver.' He won his bet.

Returning to education thereafter, Meyer built his school, working long hours and driving off to the London casinos in the evening. He hadn't bothered with sleep since the Indian uprising when hot days and noisy nights made it elusive.

From the casinos came various future parents and his one piece of advice: 'Never pass on the bank.' Doing so prematurely had once lost him Saudi Arabia.

Millfield had its stables, too, and at meetings we'd follow Meyer surreptitiously to see which of his horses he was backing.

Leaving Millfield in 1971, Meyer opened schools in Athens before failing health brought him back to Somerset a year ago.

Now he sits writing his memoirs, praising Terry Alderman, growling about English batting and bowlers who 'hit the seam and hope'.

We first met in 1969 when he gave a free education to my family and jobs to my parents. We've met regularly ever since, though upon leaving school on rather more satisfactory terms.

FRED DOVE

Last March, Frederick Dove took a slip catch off my bowling. Honestly. It was a simple chance, as these things go, though considering the bowler, slip might with reason have been dozing peacefully, confident of leading an undisturbed life.

We were playing in Khartoum, near where Lord Kitchener impressed a youthful Winston Churchill by defying overwhelming odds to quell an uprising. We were playing in shorts under a sizzling sun, and without even breaking our fast, for games are played early in Sudan, and a fellow can score 100 before downing his porridge. Local people, evidently puzzled, wondered what these demented figures were up to.

But forget about the locality. Concentrate upon Mr Dove, for within minutes he had hung on to a blinder in the gully. Summoned to the bowling crease he took a vital wicket by catching a thunderous straight drive. By nightfall he'd taken three more wickets, put a pig on a spit, and chased your correspondent around a squash court.

Pretty routine stuff? Don't you believe it. These events speak of towering courage rarely encountered in sport or anything else, for Fred – though he scarcely bothers to mention it, dismisses it as if it were the merest hindrance – is a desperately handicapped victim of thalidomide.

Barely 152cm, his arms end just below the elbow and his three-fingered hands hook back into his arms from which contorted position they cannot move. To all intents and purposes these hands render playing any game absolutely impossible. Yet Fred is a decent club cricketer who asks no quarter and gives none. Once an affection for cricket developed, nothing on earth was going to stop him playing it. Determined to stand his ground, determined to join in, to win respect, Fred simply studied the challenges, worked out ways of meeting them, and practised hard until he could compete.

To catch a ball he has to cross his hands as if they were to be tied, forming them into a cup into which the ball can drop. In the field, he scurries around on powerful legs and whips the ball back with a unique underarm action. To bowl he pushes the ball forwards from beside his ear, varying his pace and trajectory to take wickets. For batting, he thrusts his specially made handle through his hands and stands as if he were a side-on croquet player.

And it works. Fred takes his catches, regularly dismisses good batsmen and even scores runs now and then. Derek Underwood bowled to him once and, seeing him take guard, asked how he should bowl. 'Normally,' was the immediate and gruff reply from Fred's rivals and chums.

As a boy, Fred had immense difficulties, enduring three hip operations, once being in plaster for five months and each time having to learn to walk again. As an adolescent he could ignore his handicaps but was terribly embarrassed by his height and hated people talking as if he were not present, as if his brain had been damaged as well.

To win respect, to be accepted, he decided simply to be equal. Accordingly, he took up cricket and soccer and was dismayed at not being allowed to play Rugby. He found ways of competing, gripping a squash racquet halfway up, using his brain and his strength, finding what he could do and doing it well.

Hard study took him to Oxford where he played cricket for a village team and took a first class degree in modern languages. Preferring to avoid an office job he volunteered for service overseas and was sent to teach in Sudan from 1985 to 1987. Liking this chaotic, gentle African city built where the Niles meet, he decided to stay. Fred lives now with his girlfriend and an artist in a tiny, muddled flat in a back street of Khartoum, a flat different from others only in that a dove is painted on its door.

Soon it will be time for the next challenge. Already he's applied for a job with the World Service. For the present, Fred is content to teach, to administer the Sudan Club, to edit the local English newspaper, to catch his catches and to chase *Herald* writers and others around the squash courts.

If you see him do not bother to commiserate with him. For he will reply: 'There were 10,000 children of thalidomide, 3,000 of whom were stillborn. I was one of the lucky ones.' Instead, ask about his batting, for nothing is dearer to his heart than improving it. 'I want to score a 50,' he says. 'And I want to hit a six.'

Don't bet against him doing either.

MEETING VAN RIET

Jean Baptiste Van Riet is an extraordinary man. To visit him is to undertake a pilgrimage beginning in Johannesburg and ending in a dusty town set deep in the flatlands of the west South African hinterland where roads come from nowhere and are going nowhere. To such areas as these, dispossessed Boers trekked, for this is rugged thankless land where a man ekes out a living, conquering hardship, where comfort's prim offerings are seldom seen.

Excelsior has a population of 1,000–'3,000 if you include the blacks' says Ivan, an Irish barman who speaks 12 languages and warns that to knock on a black man's door is to risk a spear through the chest, reward for an invasion of territory. A fellow is supposed to shout a greeting.

This is a small town. To contact Van Riet at his farm you must crank up an old telephone, urging it to life as if it was a reluctant gramophone. A lady answers and connects the call and probably listens to it as well for in such places adventure must be found and rumours spread so that every stranger is noted and his purpose debated. Van Riet is home, remembers a mutual friend whose name I drop and says he will pick me up. Meanwhile blacks stand outside the pub and are allowed to buy Coca-Cola and beer through the backdoor. Ivan takes their money and gives the change, 'they can't add up,' he says, a point confirmed by beery Boers, Verwoerd territory this, not De Klerk, a poacher turned gamekeeper those men reckon.

Van Riet arrives wearing tennis clothes and honking his horn, a sprightly, vivacious old man of darting eyes and broad grin, a man alive, a man slower to the net these days but still capable of a cunning cross-court forehand. A farmer born and bred, he leaves the heavier work to his son who lives on their small property where wheat grows and sheep graze. Upon hearing of Ivan's opinions he laughs uproariously and says 'they see blacks only in the raw' and points towards black business magazines which he carries around in his car to show to sceptics. 'It is possible, you see. Fear itself is the enemy.' Easier to say this in Excelsior, of course, than in those squatter camps where hundreds of thousands of people are dumped, far from the prying eye, uneducated and poor masses soon to be given a vote.

Van Riet is a farmer, an Afrikaner, a member of the Dutch Reform Church, and a liberal, a real liberal, not the fairweather sort. His credentials are clear. A severe drought gripped Transvaal during the 1930s adding to the economic turmoil already crippling Western and African economies. All around him farmers tried to sjambok reluctant black workers into greater activity, a tactic which produced a sullen reaction and more sjambokking, more resentment. Van Riet had no truck with such behaviour and decided, instead, to build a reservoir the better to resist the cruel changes of climate. For five years he worked beside his labourers, stripped to the waist, hour after hour, day after day, month after month, dusty and weary. Eventually it was done, 500 yards long and 100 yards wide, a source of life, a place to hoard water against a dry season. And it still endures, though a part of a wall had crumbled a week earlier, and is still full of shining water.

Upon completing his tasks, all those years ago, Van Riet called a meeting of his men and their families and told them he was forming a committee to do the hiring and firing, and was giving them a share in the farm profits. He was offering incentives and demanding responsibility and he was trusting his black workers, a devastating change, one which sent shockwaves through a town hitherto united in its holding of the line. Equality was for the nancy-boys in the Cape.

Oh, yes, and he meant to build a school in wattle and daub for their children, a promise which was kept, like all the others.

For years thereafter whenever Van Riet ventured into town folk walked ostentatiously away and one or two spat as he went by, for traitors must pay a heavy price.

Van Riet does not talk much about these difficult times. 'It was a bad period,' is all he will say, and this without a trace of bitterness. A gregarious fellow he continued laughing and talking even if no one answered, and bore the pain manfully, refusing to regard his opponents as wicked, simply as people fearful of moving towards the light.

A man of strong conviction he stopped going to Dutch Reform

Church services because they were not open to all Christians, and attended instead an Anglican church nearby. Not that his faith changed, rather he waited for his church to catch up with him, just as he was waiting for his country. Not for a second did he consider abandoning either, though he did build a second farm just across the Limpopo, in Bechuanaland (now Botswana). His 'funk-hole' he called it, a place to run to if things really did turn nasty. Meanwhile he was timidly, terribly alone, in Excelsior. His wife, a no less courageous character, who did not share his beliefs, stood by him, suffering in silence. In time she was to be struck down by sickness and Jean Baptiste was to nurse her for 15 years, hardly leaving her side until she passed away a year ago. In his ministrations he was helped by his housekeeper, a patient black lady, one utterly faithful to her friend and employer. During those 15 years of decline Mrs Van Riet was hardly more than a stick, yet she too would not break.

When the Nationalists took power after the war Van Riet joined Alan Paton and others in forming the Liberal Party. Paton he admired enormously as a man 'you could not budge'. For this act of political challenge he was punished, police arriving from distant Pretoria to search his house and to seize his passport, dismissing his protestations that he 'is as good a South African as any of you'. His telephone was tapped, an intrusion he was powerless to resist. He said he had nothing to hide and asked why local police had not been used. Why rush hundreds of miles to turn over his humble farm? But, really, he knew the answer, understood that it was his persecutors who were scared, for their authority depended upon a silencing of unruly elements, especially whites persuaded that men be judged by the content of their character.

For twenty years he endured, toiling away on his farm and rising to be Chairman of the Liberal party in Transvaal. And then, suddenly, notoriety fell upon Excelsior. Senior officers at the local division of the Nationalist party were found to have black concubines and children by them; cheques were produced as evidence that these officials were supporting their offspring. Apartheid was, by now, in the spotlight and reporters, cameras, critics and commentators descended upon Excelsior from all parts of the globe, much to the horror of the government. It was a terrific story, one of the best, apostles of apartheid shacked up with black women! Here was hypocrisy writ large. And here was a chance for vengeance, for reporters soon heard of Van Riet's tale and accordingly were all agog to hear his opinion upon the matter. And here came Van Riet's finest hour; the hour in which he proved his greatness. For he said nothing, absolutely nothing, by way of criticism, simply shrugged his shoulders and observed that 'I am a liberal' and left it at that. Had not he wanted blacks and whites to love each other all his life? And now he was supposed to chastise? He scorned such grandstanding.

Not surprisingly the case never did see the light of day, and all of these bloodhounds packed their bags and went home. Alas, some of the officials were mortified in their shame and the chairman killed himself whilst his deputy, a butcher, narrowly failed to do so. Sadly no more money was given to their mistresses or their bastard children, who suffered accordingly.

Ever since, Van Riet on his property and Excelsior behind its barricades, have endured as before, symbols of hope and fear.

Now Van Riet was off to see if his sheep were in good fettle, and to argue once again for a country in which every adult had a say. Excelsior, of course, was worried, betrayed by a Government which it no longer trusted, fearful of a future in which men who throw spears at casual visitors are elected into government. Education is the answer, Van Riet says, and it is needed on both sides lest fear take a grip. His life has been an extraordinary testament to courage, and he may live to see his dream enacted, and to help tackle the vast difficulties which must follow. He will try to educate the blacks he meets, and Ivan too, for his need is no less great.

CONFESSIONS

ROEBUCK THE DEMON
BOWLER 2

Towards the end of May Somerset cricketers sat around in their dressing room awaiting the team talk which was to be delivered by Mr Christopher Tavaré, a monkish fellow who had earlier in his career served as a model for the painter Mr Lowry. This Tavaré was regarded as a pretty sane sort of a fellow, though Tauntonians had plans to change that because pretty sane sort of fellows are not *de rigueur* in Somerset. This Tavaré observed that we had only four bowlers left on their feet. There had been a cock-up. Marks wasn't playing and Rose had gone in the fetlock. Only four! It didn't sound many. I peered around the room. There was old Jones, our huffing fast bowler, and there, steady Mallender. Our spinner, Tim Scriven, (we were going through a period of playing obscure spinners) was over yonder which left only one fellow to be found. Everyone peered around as if they were in the House of Lords. Suddenly they looked at me. A thought struck. Good God, he means me. I am a bowler. Tavaré regards me as the team's salvation. May I tell you how this came to pass?

Until a month ago I didn't bowl at all, an entirely satisfactory arrangement in my opinion. Some wily old pros recalled a dim and distant past in which I trotted down a few innocent off-breaks but this was a period of history which I was trying to live down, as Mr Gorbachev is the Brezhnev era, as Brezhnev did the Kosygin era. I had, it is true, taken a wicket with medium pacers (that of Pringle) and with leg-spin (Sadiq) and so stood side by side with Sobers in at least one respect. But this was the sort of whimsical fact which obscures rather than informs. Having handed on the captaincy to Victor, I had pictured a pleasant interlude in which I became a grand old man who spent his time pottering down to third man, nattering with the crowd and munching the occasional daisy. Time at last to bat and to pontificate, both occupations dear to my heart.

And then I made a fatal mistake. It's funny how some pay for mistakes whilst to others they are but flea bites on an elephant's hide. It was cold, you see, and we were in Southampton. Two overs remained before we could take another new ball. (Scoring had been heavy but we were still on the reds.) I mumbled something to Victor about rolling my arm over and he considered it worth a go. I delivered a drifter. Actually it was more of a hobo, for it drifted not because it had nothing better to do, but out of definite belief. Certainly it had plenty of time to move wherever it chose. Though directed at off stump it took perverse pleasure in wandering down the pads of Mr Stephen Jefferies who, wearing several thick sweaters, contrived to miss it, a turn of events which caused wide-spread consternation and led some to appeal for a catch and others for a stumping. The latter was given. While it was too cold for anyone to appear disgruntled it cannot be said that Stephen appeared entirely gruntled by this twist of fate.

I, on the other hand, was pleased. No alarm bells rang. To my mind it was the sort of aberration reserved solely for the cruellest month. My bowling average would sink dramatically from 73 to 69, but I would not be proclaimed an all-rounder, a label I resisted as stoutly as Caesar resisted the crown (though later he probably reflected he might as well have been hung for a sheep as for a goat).

Then Glamorgan arrived in Taunton to find a turning pitch, a matter entirely unconnected with the elevation to the captaincy of our only spinner. Morris and Cann (opinion was divided whether he should be called tin or opener) batted valiantly, and after 120 overs or so Victor looked flummoxed. One of the first things learnt by a captain is to look in total command even when things are going defiantly wrong. Vic hasn't got the hang of this yet. In some agitation, he pointed out the situation, said he was flummoxed and did I fancy a bowl?

The die was cast. Morris edged what might, to the undiscriminating eye, have looked like a half volley to slip. North fell to one which might, from a distance, be thought to have pitched a trifle short. I took two wickets.

Sussex were our next opponents and Vic put me on again, though I had not considered donning bowling boots to be necessary that day. It was a greenish pitch and only later did I realise that Victor had meant me to bowl my funny little seamers rather than my funny little cutters. Undeterred he called upon me to deliver the final seven overs of the Sunday League game, and a hectic run chase ended in a tied match.

There was no end to it. And what, pray, do I bowl? In truth my style is still at the experimental stage. It is possible, I admit, that one or two refinements may be needed. They are called quick off-breaks, not because they are quick, not because they turn, but because that is what is sent down from my end. What happens all those yards away is none of my business. Tactics are, in fact, my only weapon, confusing the batsman my only threat. To this end I do not mark out a run and whistle through the overs so quickly that the batsman has no time to consider the drivel being served up. If, perchance, he is an impressionable youngster I try to look sage, as if I have something up my sleeve. Actually this is not difficult. My life has been ruined by the fact that people think I'm plotting something even on those rare occasions when I'm not.

Anyhow I now take the field in my bowling boots, and I have a sore spinning finger, which might surprise some batsmen. DeFreitas and Mark Taylor were my next victims. DeFreitas fell in the leg trap which was located at deep mid-wicket. Taylor hit a short one to cover. Then came two more wickets against Essex at Chelmsford, John Stephenson and Paul Prichard, followed by the last over drama in the B&H quarter-final against the Universities at Taunton. Can it last? Why not? The youngsters think I'm up to something, and the old 'uns dare not get out to me. It'll last as long as any other bluff, I'd say.

ROEBUCK THE
SECRET AGENT

Everything is going according to plan. Unless dreadful blunders are made I will, by the time the trees begin to cry, have helped England to hold the Ashes. But, soft, I hear you say, this fellow has never played for England, not even last year when nearly everyone else did, so what contribution can he have made? A subtle and devious one, a voice, mine, replies.

As a boy I had only one ambition. I wanted to lead England to victory in an Ashes series. Heavens, I'd captained the Glastonbury Under-13s so it wasn't much to ask, besides which, as far as I could see, beating Australia was a piece of cake. Get Bill Lawry out and you were through 'em.

Naturally, as England captain I'd run the country in my spare time, which was what the captains of my youth appeared to do. Ted Dexter and Richie Benaud certainly did. Experience of this cruel world had broken most childhood illusions but, frankly, I'd take some convincing this one was wrong.

Years rolled by and the call never came. Most of my friends had a stab at the job but I was ignored. Apparently the selectors were looking for a chap rather closer in character to Mr Henry Blofeld, a dear fellow but something of a patrician.

Finally, an hour of enlightenment arrived and I realised the fault was mine. I had been born only fairly great. Moreover it dawned upon me that my chances of achieving greatness were slim and I could not foresee it being thrust upon me. The crooked, warted finger of grim obscurity beckoned.

This was a blow. Many a man would have buckled. I confess I did, for a time, take to drinking gin with my breakfast cereal. I did, for a time, indulge in wagering upon the outcome of horse races. I even began to read the novels of Mr Jeffrey Archer. And then, salvation. Wandering brokenly through the back streets of Soho, I bumped into someone from Lord's.

Over a glass of milk I told my tale. Being a brilliant scholar – a qualification essential in cricket's inner-sanctum – he immediately found a solution. I could still do my bit by going behind enemy lines. Fly to Australia, he advised, and teach their children how to bat – if that didn't finish 'em off nothing would.

Though I say it, who shouldn't, I had found my destiny. At once, I began running cricket camps and coaching school teams. Within months half of Sydney was sweeping good length deliveries and blocking full tosses. It was uncanny·how they took to it. For decades antipodean fast bowlers and legspinners had been thorns in England's side. I did away with both of 'em.

Open your eyes and everywhere you will see evidence of my work.

I had one great stroke of luck. Even before I arrived, things were only going tolerably well in Australia. A chap called Kerry Packer was having a row with some delightful old buffers. He wanted to poke 'em in the eye. Some cricketers took his side merely because they'd been paid a pittance for decades. I could not see what the fuss was about. England's cricketers had been paid miserably for years and they hadn't complained.

This Packer had begun a game which rather cunningly, I thought, he called cricket, although in no way did it resemble the original. Players ran around in funny clothes, white balls were used, games were staged at night, drinks arrived on a scooter and a vast screen replayed interesting moments, none of which happened at Lord's. Naturally, the old-timers objected to all this, so when things began to go wrong – a decline entirely due to my efforts – Packer was blamed. He was, and is, the perfect alibi. Mind you, his son – craftily called Dean Jones – was a nuisance. He could bat.

With Packer's help, things were moving along nicely. London was happy. Telegrams arrived when Graham Yallop was appointed captain, and when Kim Hughes resigned and left on a jet plane.

And then a fearful rumpus arose. Australia had found a cricketer. Some bloke called Waugh. Apparently there was a whole tribe of 'em. How had they slipped through the net? It was beyond understanding. Something had to be done. A thought struck. They do, from time to time. He'd survived on his own soil. What if we took him to England?

It seemed certain to work. By golly, I gave it my best shot. Having enticed him to Somerset I went so far as to give the poor fellow some advice, a move which had never previously failed.

Incredibly, Waugh survived even this. We'll get him in the end, though.

My work continues. In fact it is spreading. Cricket camps were not enough. Nobbling Steve Waugh was not enough. I had to creep into every nook and cranny of Australian cricket. I had to join the august, sober and incorruptible body of men, the Australian cricket writing fraternity.

Now, I prattle about all manner of nonsense, as one or two readers have been kind enough to point out, and it is studied as if Moses himself were the author. Some colleagues – notably Ian Chappell and Bill Lawry – have seen through my game, but they are voices in the wilderness. Australia is capitulating. Under my guidance they pick the wrong teams, elect the wrong leaders and enact the worst possible laws. Again, open your eyes, the evidence is all around.

Can you any longer attribute Australia's impending defeat to any other source? Is this not the work of a master?

All the Englishmen have to do is administer the *coup de grâce*. But cricket is unreliable and precautions must be taken. Accordingly, when Allan Border appears in Taunton, I'll take him aside and offer words of advice. When it comes to winning the Ashes, it does not pay to take risks.

A TEAM TALK

SUDDENLY there is a flash of lightning and tremors slide down everyone's backbone. Our leader arises to speak to his assembled crew. A hush rolls around the room, for our captain is a formidable man. Heads hang low for fear of meeting him eye to eye. Like a Gestapo interrogator, his eye strips you naked, revealing all. Moments of horror creep back to mind. That time I had an appalling slog just after the leader had ordered me to 'get your head down, lad, and keep it down'. It all comes back. Does his roving, bloodshot eye see it?

He stands on the table now, arms aloft like the start of a Columbia film. He pauses, though he has not yet begun. The hush deepens into gloom. They say that evangelical preachers in the South create unfathomable pitches of silence before the haranguing begins. Our leader glares around him, slowly rolling his eyes. Foam seeps from the corner of his mouth. He sees into the darkest reaches, not a nook nor a cranny escapes. Shiftless souls who seek solitary seats emerge from the shadows to face the storm.

How will he begin, we wonder? No, not 'Friends, team, countrymen!' We had that last week. Nor 'Awake, arise or be for ever fall'n'. That would be too much, even for him. After all, it's only the lunch interval and they are 68 for 4. Maybe he'll sing 'Stand up and fight, men, fight for your lives'. Surely not – more likely 'Examine yourselves, examine your consciences, examine your performances'. That has a chance, a good Churchillian ring to it, and he hasn't used it for a day or two.

How does he view the morning's play, I wonder? His upper lip is curling, obviously he is not happy. Before the game he announced that the wicket 'is a line and length wicket', that 'we've got to bowl straight', that 'each of you must face your responsibilities', that 'you must keep your eye on me in the field', that 'if we can get the first five out we're through the beggars', that 'this is the most important game in the club's history' and that 'you've got to be mean'. After this, the boot-stamping, the Taunton war-dance and then onto the field.

I did my best. I mean to say, it would have been a helluva catch. I was alert, fit, keen as mustard. So I dropped the ruddy thing. So what? No-one's perfect. I'd like to have seen him catch it. He'd say he'd have caught it 'between the cheeks of his backside'. He probably would have done, too.

And as for that one that slipped through my legs, well I had no chance with that. No chance at all. Bad bounce, rough outfield, spinning ball, fierce hit, no chance. So why did he pucker his eyelids as he swept past me around the room? What about Vic's effort the other day? I mean, it's not for me to criticise, I don't suppose, but it was a pretty tame effort; he could easily have caught it if he'd moved, if he was not so dozy first thing in the morning. Has he forgotten about that? I doubt it: for heaven's sake, he still remembers the four overthrows I gave away five years ago. Five years ago! We all make mistakes, these things are unavoidable, aren't they? We're only human, so you've got to be tolerant.

Oh dear. Our leader is not looking terribly tolerant. He's never thought much of namby-pamby, lily-livered liberals. He's glaring at Bill. What's Bill done? Oh hell, yes, now that really was a cock-up. He should have been backing up, he should have stopped the shy at the stumps. Yes, that was pretty poor, I'm bound to admit. He's got every right to bring that one up. Poor old Bill, he'll be on the lino (we can't afford carpet) in a minute.

He's opening his lips! My goodness, here we go, over the top, lads, all aboard. I bet he speaks well. Not as well as at Chelmsford maybe. That really was a speech. Lloyd George, Hamlet, Oscar Wilde, none of 'em could have matched it. Dame Edith Evans perhaps, but then she was a lady and they have an advantage: just look at Boadicea and Joan of Arc if you doubt it. Chelmsford was a peak. He spoke in an old-fashioned way, varying his voice from boom to hiss, throwing his metaphors into the far recesses of the dingy changing room. What was it he said? 'Now we are engaged in a great battle, testing whether this county can long endure. We meet on the great battlefield of Chelmsford. The world will little note, nor long remember what we do here. It is rather for us to be dedicated to the great task before us, that we here highly resolve that ex-Somerset players shall not have played in vain.' That's what I call a team talk! No-one knew what on earth he was on about, of course, but it felt impressive: as Macmillan said when Khrushchev ranted and raved, banging his fists on the table and shouting, 'I've got no idea what he's saying, but he seems to mean it!'

Is that steam coming out of his ears? Certainly his nostrils are twitching and his neck is reddening. I suppose captains need a bit of fire. Jeeves couldn't inspire a team, nor could Hamlet. Too much low-key wisdom on the one hand, too much dithering on the other. It's no use some nice chap saying, 'Right, chaps, we're in a bit of a pickle. The oppo are on top, lads, so let's try jolly hard.' Or even worse, 'Well, chaps, it's a nice day. Things aren't going too well, so let's at least enjoy the sun, the trees and the twittering birds.' No, that sort of stuff doesn't work – too weak-kneed. Our leader's right, really. You feel like those devils in *Paradise Lost* after our leader has spoken:

> They heard and were abash't, and up they sprang
> Upon the wing as men wont to watch
> On duty, sleeping, found by whom they dread
> Raise and bestir themselves ere well awake.
> Nor did they not perceive the evil plight
> In which they were, or the fire's powers not feel.

That's the idea. Good *Land of Hope and Glory* stuff, still ringing in your ears as you take the field with confident step.

The pause is over, his throat is moving. He speaks, yes, he speaks. 'Umpires in the middle,' yells our twelfth man, with the timing of a Groucho Marx. Our leader appears angry, as an actor might if the theatre catches fire just as he is launching into his first 'To be or not to be'. Now we'll never hear that speech. Or maybe we will. At teatime.

ROEBUCK'S MAXIMS

Cricket

TRADITIONALLY, cricket has been a game lacking in thoroughness and American proficiency. None of the efficient countries seem to play it. At Somerset we used to have a medium-pacer called Burgess. He came in one day and said: 'You know what my wife's done? She's put me on a diet. I can only have seven roast potatoes for lunch now.'

It is a cussed game. It can show you glimpses of beauty in a stroke perfectly played, perhaps, and then it throws you back into the trough of mediocrity.

County cricket is rather like trench warfare at times; the qualities you most need to survive are graft and endurance.

One day cricket thrives upon fervour. It creates climaxes, whereas Test cricket is a slow unwinding of duels between cricketers. In Tests, the players dictate the course of the game: in one day cricket, the game is the boss.

Perhaps cricket is more like boxing than any other sport in the way it transcends mere technical mastery and requires hidden gifts of timing and judgement.

Cricketers

A cricketer, if he is not around the bend, is at least fast approaching the corner.

Somerset's county team includes a Shakespearean actor, a man who keeps a ferret, a couple of authors, and a bloke who knocks down churches in the winter.

The idea of finding a successful formula sustains cricketers as the belief in Eldorado sustained explorers.

Some players manage to defy statistics by being either 'promising' or 'about to retire' or else contributing something mystical off the field – being a good clubman, an ambassador, etc. But ultimately cricketers flourish or fail on the evidence of their records. Oh yes, you've got to give them figures.

Cricket is full of introverts who find the game itself intensely challenging and utterly frustrating but who feel ill at ease in front of the public.

Off-spinners are usually fairly sane characters. Left-arm spinners and leg-spinners are mostly crackpots.

Personal Approach

To me, cricket is a battle with the self; whenever I bat I feel ridiculous temptations I must restrain. The season is a five-month fight to play only strokes that are intelligently calculated.

Early in my career I went through a terrible slump. Nothing seemed to work. One day a Somerset supporter, a farmer, took me aside and said: 'We're worried about you, because you aren't trying.' I was quite shaken and replied: 'What's the price of wheat?'. I went off. 'Bugger it,' I thought, 'if they think I'm not trying I won't try.' The next day I went into bat and scored 63 in 31 minutes. Later, the same fellow came back to me and said: 'I knew after our little chat you'd do well.'

. . . Warner banged one down and before I could think better of it I had whacked it through mid-wicket to the fence. Must stop doing that somehow. It isn't a good business shot for me.

Last year when I hit a six in a John Player League game, a spectator called out, 'Good Lord, I've seen it all now.'

It's very hard to dissociate one's human worth and one's success with a lump of wood in one's hand.

In form I know that the best way of scoring runs is to be myself, and I have the confidence to believe that this will be good enough.

Teams

Cricket is a team game. The purpose of the team, however, is not to be harmonious but to succeed. Harmony is not an end in itself; it is merely a means to an end.

Only pride was at stake this afternoon as it turned out. But perhaps pride is the sharpest weapon a team can have.

Being dropped and rested is, like getting a hiding at school, the sort of thing that sounds a pretty good idea for everyone else.

A good team needs a hard core of experienced cricketers around whom the novices learn their trade.

Two things are being said about this West Indian side. One is that it is too old. The other is that it is too young. As a piece of optimism this ranks with the gentleman who went to England without his umbrella.

Richards and Botham

When Richards bothers to take singles, bowlers know they are in for a hard day.

Perhaps that straight bat is why Richards has, I think, the best defence I've ever seen.

At times Viv provokes fast bowlers to do their damnedest. Facing Len Pascoe in Sydney, he hooked a mighty boundary and replied to Pascoe's lethal glare with a teasing 'Butter, Lennie, butter.' Next ball a vicious bouncer was cracked for six, and Pascoe's comments were cut short by Richards: 'Marmalade, Lennie, marmalade!'

Botham and Queensland were made for each other – big, brassy, noisy and aggressively masculine.

Botham is a man who would have charged at the head of the Light Brigade, but he is also a man who might have issued the order.

When I was out, Richards was joined by Botham, who had taken a terrible pasting from the papers after his dismissal yesterday. As we crossed I nearly said, 'Good luck, but for Pete's sake don't try that back-handed sweep,' but thought I'd better not. Botham broke his duck inevitably with that stroke and proceeded to pound 85 in 13 overs, adding 138 in that time with Richards. There wasn't much Nottinghamshire could do; these two seemed able to hit leg-side yorkers from Hadlee over third man if they chose.

Spectators

English crowds are like sherry. West Indian crowds are like rum. Australian crowds are like Fosters.

There is nothing in cricket more calculated to raise a laugh than the sight of some determined and serious man under a spiralling catch.

An image persists of Henry Blofeld cracking champagne bottles and entertaining blondes until the early hours, and arriving at the game with a stinking headache. Really, of course, he snuggles up every night with a hot-water bottle, reading one of the novels of William Makepeace Thackeray.

Microphones do funny things to people. You find yourself babbling away and sometimes are just as puzzled as the listener as to how the sentence is going to end.

It's appalling how many of your most private mannerisms are caught, exaggerated even, by television.

Today's cricket was played in front of a disappointing crowd, enlivened only by hordes of schoolboys who were there, presumably, by way of punishment.

Observations

Sport is not merely for exercise; it is its own pursuit of perfection.

The ability that counts is the ability to improve and to continue improving.

To be an aggressive player you have to be a man with no regrets.

Fortune does not favour the brave; it favours the sane.

Greatness can include a talent for letting an opponent destroy himself.

Captaincy seems to include half-hearing conversations which you'd far rather not hear at all. Sitting in the gents this afternoon at a critical stage of our recovery, I thought I heard someone say that a wicket had fallen. I rushed matters in hand to see if this could be true ... The conversation, it emerged, had been between two gentlemen I didn't recognise upon some unknown topic. Captains, I assume, are haunted by the ever-looming prospect of collapse, and hear the phrase 'another wicket gone' in every conversation.

Inner rings are splendid for those within them.

Achievements in concrete are too often mistaken for concrete achievements.

They had built the wall and felt they had the right to knock it down (Somerset 1986).

Learning how to use a machine is no substitute for education.

Loyalty is a slippery word. The truth is disloyal to those served by lies.

ACKNOWLEDGEMENTS

The author and publisher thank the following for permission to reprint material previously published:

Allen and Unwin for 'Something Fell from Heaven', 'Brian Close', 'My Only Cricket Riot', 'In Fiji', 'Roebuck the Demon Bowler 1 (Kowloon)', 'The Long Black Telegraph Pole', 'A Team Talk' from *Slices of Cricket* 1982; Allen and Unwin for 'A Precarious Preoccupation' from *It Never Rains* 1984; Kingswood Press for 'The Art of Cricket' from *Ashes to Ashes* 1987; the *Sydney Morning Herald* for 'Cricket in a Cow Paddock', 'Charging at Windmills', 'The Team for Venus', 'Larwood's Legacy', 'Gavaskar', 'Border', 'Dean Jones (1 & 2)', 'Cricket's Lethal Bomb', 'A Perfumed Harlot', 'In Praise of Sportsmanship', 'Sammy Woods', 'Whatever Happened to Otto Nothling?', 'The Tough Bit', 'Chee Quees', 'Peter McWhinney', 'R. J. O. Meyer – Cad, Genius and Fox', 'Fred Dove'; *The Sunday Times* for 'Hadlee the Lean Machine', 'Boycott', 'Stephen Waugh', 'Australia versus England, Second Test at Perth, November 1986', 'Australia versus England, Bicentenary Test at Sydney, January 1988', 'Time to Bite the South African Bullet', 'The Carrot', 'Why the Captain Lay Down and Cried', 'Botham in 1985', 'Still the Greatest'; *The Sunday Times* magazine for 'Gatting'; *The Cricketer* for 'Great Sir Garfield', 'Roebuck the Demon Bowler 2'; *Time Out* (UK) for 'Botham the Man'; Channel 9 Ashes Brochure for 'Roebuck the Secret Agent'.